AMERICA
IN THE
20TH
CENTURY

1940-1949

AMERICA
IN THE
20TH
CENTURY

SECOND EDITION
Revised and Expanded with Primary Sources

1940-1949

Kelli Peduzzi

MARSHALL CAVENDISH
NEW YORK • LONDON • TORONTO • SYDNEY

Marshall Cavendish
99 White Plains Road
Tarrytown, NY 10591

Website: www.marshallcavendish.com

Library of Congress Cataloging-in-Publication Data

America in the 20th Century.-- 2nd ed., rev. and expanded with primary sources.
     p. cm.
   Includes bibliographical references and index.
   ISBN 0-7614-7364-5 (set)
   1. United States -- Civilization -- 20th century. I. Title: America in the twentieth century.
   E169.1.A471872   2003
   973.9--dc21

                                    2001052949

   ISBN 0-7614-7369-6 (vol. 5)

Printed in Malaysia
Bound in the United States of America

06 05 04 03 02   5 4 3 2 1

Series created by Discovery Books

Series Editor: Paul Humphrey
Academic Consultants: Gregory Bush,
Chair of History Department, University of Miami, Coral Gables
Richard J. Taylor, History Department, University of Wisconsin, Parkside
Marshall Cavendish Editor: Peter Mavrikis
Marshall Cavendish Production Manager: Alan Tsai
Project Editors: Valerie Weber and Yvonne Rees
Picture Research: Gillian Humphrey
Design concept: Laurie Shock
Designers: Ian Winton and Winsome Malcolm

*(Frontispiece) "Hasten the Homecoming — Buy Victory Bonds," was a typical Norman Rockwell
Saturday Evening Post cover from World War II.*

Contents

CHAPTER 1
A Shadow Across the Future

German leader Adolf Hitler addresses a massed gathering of Nazi troops at Nuremberg in 1936. Each September from 1933 to 1938, Hitler's propaganda minister, Josef Goebbels, organized a giant rally of the German National Socialist (Nazi) party at Nuremberg. Germany's totalitarian regime was soon to burst its borders, overwhelming Poland before turning on Belgium, Holland, and France.

The 1940s and the decade preceding were some of the grimmest years in U.S. history. In the 1930s, the Great Depression had shaken the U.S. economy to its core and with it, Americans' faith in their democratic system. On the heels of this crisis came World War II in 1939. Nazi Germany's dictator, Adolf Hitler, had begun his conquest of western Europe and changed the balance of power throughout the world. Freedom and prosperity had never seemed so fragile as they did at the dawn of the new decade, and the national mood was far from hopeful.

By 1937, the severe economic convulsions brought on by the Great Depression had subsided slightly, though the country was in a recession and unemployment remained high. Unemployment had shrunk to 15 percent from a peak of 25 percent in 1933, but this was not enough to lift America out of its grim mood. True, President Franklin D. Roosevelt's New Deal had used taxpayers' dollars to put millions of people to work for the federal government, constructing dams, highways, bridges, buildings, and organizing arts projects for the Works Progress Administration (WPA). But as the new decade approached, more than eight million

people out of a total U.S. population of 132 million were still without a job.

Disillusionment with the New Deal ran high as America failed to recover. Millions were still jobless, homeless, and hungry. The American dream became out of reach of many ordinary Americans.

Rising Fear

Along with this disillusionment came an undercurrent of fear, particularly among better-off white Americans. President Roosevelt's relief programs seemed dangerously radical. Some saw the New Deal as thinly veiled socialism. They feared that with America's crumbling capitalist economy and the rise of communism and fascism abroad, democracy could not survive.

As the United States watched Germany and Italy grow stronger under fascism, American weaknesses seemed more pronounced. In response, Congress established the House Un-American Activities Committee (HUAC) in 1938 to investigate reports, most unfounded, of both Communist and Fascist subversion in the United States. But the average family was simply too worried about surviving from paycheck to paycheck to give much attention to theories of Communist conspiracy.

The Great Depression had altered the nation. Job security, not affluence, was the main goal of most Americans. Most people wanted a government that would cushion the hard blow struck by the sour economy. Laws were passed guaranteeing a minimum wage for workers, Social Security, collective bargaining for labor, the five-day work week, stricter child labor laws, and banking reforms. These laws remain an important part of the American system today.

During the thirties, people craving a cheap escape from their troubles listened to the radio and attended the movies in huge numbers. Americans listened an average of 4.5 hours per day to adventure shows such as "The Lone Ranger" and "Buck Rogers in the Twenty-fifth Century" and the comedy and variety of Jack Benny, George Burns, and Gracie Allen. With sound, movies had become glamorous extravaganzas offering audiences a respite from their worries, and movie revenues soared to an all-time high. In 1939, the decade culminated in the epic Civil War film, *Gone with the Wind*. Running 222 minutes and costing $5 million, it was the longest and most expensive movie to have been made until then.

In the thirties, America's evolution from a nation of small rural towns to a nation of urban centers had gained speed as more mechanized farming and the Depression lured displaced country dwellers to the cities in search of work. Cities became glutted with slums and poverty. Suburbs had just begun to ring the cities as WPA-built highways opened America up to car travel as never before.

African-Americans suffered acutely during the difficult thirties, long before any civil rights legislation existed. Many individuals and institutions alike displayed an appalling willingness to separate people on the basis of skin color alone, and in many states, segregated schools, churches, public transportation, even public toilets were not only common, they were the law. Not until 1941, the year the U.S. entered World War II, would

"We want war!"

Joachim von Ribbentrop, Hitler's foreign minister, speaking to Italy's foreign minister on August 11, 1939

While the rest of the world was preparing to fight Hitler's racist tyranny, African-Americans were still waiting for the change to come. Segregated drinking fountains were standard in the Deep South.

"While we are in complete sympathy with the negro, it is against company policy to employ them as aircraft workers or mechanics . . . regardless of their training. . . . There will be some jobs as janitors for negroes."

President of the North American Aviation Co., quoted in "Negroes in the Defense Emergency" by Herbert Garfinkel

President Roosevelt establish the Fair Employment Practices Commission. African-Americans had threatened to march on Washington in August 1941 to draw attention to civil rights, but this early effort at civil rights protest did not even begin to remedy the inequities of racial injustice.

If anything, the late thirties and early forties were a time of increasing racism and antisemitism — for immigrants as well as for African-Americans and American Jews. Isolationist sentiment had taken a firm hold of the public. Immigration quotas were established, limiting the number of people who could come from each country. Even with the horrific evidence of Hitler's extermination of European Jews, for example, Congress refused to allow an additional ten thousand Jewish children to emigrate to America and escape the horrors inflicted by the Nazis.

Isolationism Grows

Preoccupied with troubles at home, the United States had turned inward in the thirties, refusing to become involved in the ominous events across the Atlantic. Though Americans roundly condemned aggressive actions such as Japan's invasion of China in 1931-1932, Hitler's rearming of the Rhine, Italy's conquest of Ethiopia, and the Spanish Civil War, these were all distant, rather unreal events in the lives of Americans. Indeed, Congress showed its fierce isolationism in 1937, passing the Joint Neutrality Resolution designed to prevent the president from involving U.S. forces in foreign conflicts, and to bar the president from selling arms to America's allies.

But the catastrophe that became World War II swallowed the entire

Many prominent Americans wanted nothing to do with the war. Among them was the popular aviator, Charles Lindbergh, who had thrilled Americans with his pioneering transatlantic flight in 1927. Here, he urges a crowd gathered on Soldiers Field, Chicago, on August 4, 1940, to "take the lead in offering a plan for peace."

world and with it, America's determined innocence. Viewing the late thirties from today's vantage point, America's entry into the war seemed all but inevitable, though it did not seem so at the time. Many, such as the staunch isolationists of the America First Committee, campaigned to keep the United States out of war. Even popular aviator Charles Lindbergh scoured the country, calling for cooperation with Germany. But the war sent shock waves around the globe that could not fail to reach U.S. shores. By the time the conflict ended, more than fifty nations were drawn in. A total of eighty million men were at arms, and fifty million military and civilian personnel died in the six years of the war.

Yet in the beginning, when faced with no clear threat to U.S. security from the Japan-Italy-Germany Axis, America dug in its heels and refused to enter the fray. Isolationism held the day in Congress. The economic woes

of the Great Depression were one reason, but two other key factors deterred the United States from entering the war. One was that Americans dreaded the prospect of repeating the carnage and debt of World War I, in which around 115,000 U.S. soldiers died on the battlefield or of disease, many more were wounded, and billions of dollars in war debts were incurred. The other, and perhaps more fatal, error was that, despite all the signs to the contrary, America simply refused to believe that Hitler meant business.

President Roosevelt, however, suspected otherwise. As early as 1937, he warned that "war is a contagion whether it be declared or not," suggesting that Hitler's seizing of the Rhineland in the name of German *Lebensraum*, or "living room," not only would continue, but must be stopped by allied opposition to him. Congress replied that Roosevelt was a

The first German tanks cross a river and enter Polish territory in September 1939. This act brought America's long-time ally, Britain, into World War II. Poland was to be divided between Germany and the Soviet Union, which was allied with the Nazis in the opening years of the war.

warmonger, and the American public wanted no part of war, so the president backed off. Still, he sensed what was coming, and for the next several years, he tried to help America's European allies where he could, despite the neutrality law restraining his powers to do so. His efforts moved the country gradually to a state of near-readiness for war.

On September 1, 1939, Hitler invaded Poland, then divided it with the Soviet Union in the infamous Non-aggression Pact — a pact that outlined the Soviet Union's plans for increasing its territory and influence over the next five decades. Hitler had already acquired, by threats of invasion, the Sudetenland (a predominantly German section of Czechoslovakia taken from Germany after World War I in the Treaty of Versailles) and, in a bloodless coup known as the *Anschluss,* Austria. The United States looked the other way, hoping these minor territories would

appease Hitler's hunger for land. Then, early in 1940, Norway, Finland, Denmark, Belgium, the Netherlands, and France were taken virtually unopposed by the seemingly unstoppable German and Soviet forces.

Now Britain was left to face the invader alone. And yet, even in the face of the gravest danger to its closest ally, the U.S. still refused to enter the war. It was a full year and a half after the surrender of Paris to the Nazis that America finally entered the war. But it took the surprise bombing of the naval base at Pearl Harbor, Hawaii, on December 7, 1941, by the Japanese, and the subsequent loss of thousands of American lives, to push the U.S. over the edge.

The Birth of the Atomic Age

Meanwhile, on January 13, 1939, the first nuclear fission of uranium atoms had been performed and correctly interpreted by two German refugee physicists, Lise Meitner and Otto Frisch, in Copenhagen, Denmark. Copied by scientists worldwide, their experiments soon led scientist Enrico Fermi in Chicago to imagine a nuclear chain reaction and the possibility of a powerful bomb that Fermi calculated would be twenty million times more powerful than TNT. Another refugee from Nazi persecution, the physicist Albert Einstein, brought the potential danger of nuclear fission to the attention of President Roosevelt. With the knowledge that Europe's largest uranium source was in Czechoslovakia (now in Nazi hands) came the fear that the Nazis might also be able to develop a nuclear bomb. To prevent this from happening — but also to explore the potential for making nuclear bombs on U.S. soil — FDR set up the Advisory Committee on Uranium on October 11, 1939, later renamed the Manhattan Project in 1941. The atomic age had dawned.

Another technological leap in the late thirties — one that would alter American culture and society forever — was the development of television. Still in its infancy, television was both a wonder and a dream that lay beyond the reach of most Americans. Very few people had sets in their homes, and very few stations existed to broadcast to those who did. But by 1939, televisions could be purchased, and in that year Franklin D. Roosevelt became the first president ever to appear on TV — at the opening ceremonies of the New York World's Fair in June. Roosevelt had already mastered the medium of radio and knew how to manipulate it to his advantage. With television, he sensed a new frontier about to open. The war naturally interrupted developments in television technology. Not until 1948 did TV experience its first full season of programming. But in 1940, with America on the brink of war, the dawn of an atomic age already breaking, and the all-seeing eye of television ready to introduce America's living rooms to a world it had tried so hard to ignore, the nation was poised for tremendous change.

"It may be possible to set up a nuclear reaction in uranium by which vast amounts of power could be released. . . . This new phenomenon would also lead to the construction of . . . extremely powerful bombs of a new type. A single bomb of this type, carried by boat and exploded in a port, might very well destroy the whole port together with some of the surrounding territory. However, such bombs might very well prove to be too heavy for transportation by air."

Albert Einstein in a letter to FDR

Renowned silent-film actor and fierce opponent of Nazism, Charlie Chaplin used humor to bring home the message to Americans — that Hitler and Italy's Mussolini were madmen who should be driven from the face of the earth. Here, Chaplin engages in pasta slapstick with Jack Oakie in the 1940 movie, The Great Dictator.

CHAPTER 2
The World at War

The Roots of War

The seeds of World War II were sown in the aftermath of World War I, during the drafting of the Treaty of Versailles, signed on June 28, 1919. Though the spark that started World War I had been ignited in Yugoslavia, the war escalated because of decades-old treaties that required other European nations to enter the fray. At war's end, the victors expected Germany — the primary combatant — to repay them for their losses.

The terms of payment were stiff. Not only did the victors demand that Germany admit its guilt for the war, return the disputed Alsace-Lorraine region to France, and turn over its African and Middle Eastern colonies to the Allies, they also wanted Germany to pay war reparations to the Allies amounting to tens of billions of dollars. The Versailles treaty also severely limited German rearmament, and it allowed the Allies to take temporary control of the German economy. The United States did not approve of this approach to international relations and refused to either ratify the treaty or join the League of Nations that had pushed for it.

The Versailles treaty was a heavy burden for the Germans to bear, both economically and emotionally. But what made Versailles most unbearable was the way it changed Germany's boundaries. Two huge empires, the former Austro-Hungarian Empire and the German Empire, were carved up into parcels now named Germany, Yugoslavia, Czechoslovakia, Poland, Hungary, and Austria. The great German Empire ceased to exist, and what's more, Germans were being made to pay for the privilege. German resentment ran deep.

In such a climate, a nationalistic fanatic like Adolf Hitler found fertile ground for his goal: to restore Germany to greatness at any cost.

Hitler Takes Power

Starting in 1934, Hitler declared Germany's obligations under the Versailles treaty to be null. He bit off little pieces of Europe — the Sudetenland in Czechoslovakia, the Rhineland, and Austria — while the rest of Europe looked the other way, hoping he would be satisfied with these seemingly insignificant territories. They reasoned that since they themselves did not yet have the military resources to wage another war, Germany could not possibly be strong enough either. And they were almost right.

Germany was indeed too weak to fight, and Hitler knew this. He further sensed the German people's anti-war mood. But he also knew that most Germans passionately hated the Weimar Republic — established by the Allies in 1919 after World War I, and Germany's only attempt at democracy up to that time — and blamed it for Germany's embarrassing defeat as well as for the current economic disaster. Most Germans craved

> *"Miserable and degenerate criminals! The more I tried to achieve clarity on the monstrous event in this hour, the more the shame of indignation and disgrace burned my brow. What was all the pain in my eyes compared to this misery?"*
>
> Adolf Hitler in *Mein Kampf,* reacting to the German government's acceptance of the peace treaty of Versailles

By gearing the nation for war, Hitler restored both Germany's economy and its national pride. Here, he reviews the largest military parade to be held in the capital, Berlin, since World War I. Nearly 300 two-man tanks, together with scores of large and medium tanks, pay homage to the Führer to honor his forty-seventh birthday on April 20, 1936.

a return to strong military leadership, which, though it meant giving up most of their personal freedom, also gave them relative prosperity and security. After all, rearming Germany would put lots of people back to work, and it held out the hope of restoring Germany to its position of military power — two prospects that convinced most Germans to give Hitler their support.

This was the atmosphere in which Hitler formed the Nazi party and gained a majority in the *Reichstag,* Germany's parliament. Once in the majority, Hitler and his party worked quickly to issue decrees, all under the terms of the Weimar constitution, with the intention of securing absolute power. In 1933, in one of history's great ironies, the German people legally gave absolute power to Hitler, and they did so under the laws of the Weimar Republic they so detested.

The Road to War

Certainly, if the people were willing to elect Hitler, the Allies were not about to go against the German will. And so, bent on the total conquest of Europe, Hitler bought time to get his war machine up and running by preaching a message of disarmament and peace to the world. Pacified, though still suspicious, the Allies left Hitler alone, busying themselves with their own internal problems, military unreadiness being one of them. Yet had the Allies heeded the warning signals, most notably Hitler's refusal to repay the billions of dollars in war costs to the Allies, and had they chosen to fulfill their own treaty obligations to keep the military expansion of Germany in check, war might have been avoided. But by the time Hitler invaded Poland on September 1,

WORLD WAR II

For further information see primary source entries on pages

11: 1556-65, 1567-70

1939, it was too late for any nation to do anything but react.

All over the world, political conflicts had been getting more and more violent. In 1936, Hitler had remilitarized the Rhineland, citing a French-Russian alliance as a threat to German borders. Soviet dictator Stalin had begun to purge some ten million Soviet citizens as threats to his power. Generalissimo Francisco Franco's Fascist rebels attacked the leftist Republic in Spain. Japan invaded China, citing the threat of communism at its borders. And Benito Mussolini, Fascist dictator in Italy, seized Ethiopia. In March 1938, Hitler seized Austria in a bloodless coup. Yet the United States viewed these ominous goings-on rather distantly. Indeed, in 1938, 59 percent of all Americans approved of British Prime Minister Neville Chamberlain's dealing away the Sudetenland to Germany in exchange for Hitler's empty promises of peace.

Clearly, no one had read *Mein Kampf,* Hitler's political testimonial, or if they had read it, they didn't take it seriously. In his book, which was published in the 1920s, Hitler imagined a Germany that engulfed all of Europe and made slaves of the conquered. By the 1930s, he had achieved the first step by flexing his political muscles with other European powers and using armed intimidation by his Nazi storm-troopers. Hardly a shot had been fired and he was already taking control.

Rapidly, it became clear that Austria and the Sudetenland would not be enough for Hitler. In March 1939, he invaded and occupied the rest of Czechoslovakia. Hitler then turned his sights on Poland, claiming Germany's right to certain Polish lands. Germany invaded Poland on September 1, 1939, and divided it with the Soviet Union. Within days of the invasion, Britain and France declared

> "We have sustained a total and unmitigated defeat. . . . Do not blind ourselves to that. . . . And do not suppose that this is the end. This is only the beginning of the reckoning. This is only the first sip, the first foretaste of a bitter cup which will be proffered to us year by year unless, by a supreme recovery of moral health and martial vigor, we arise again and take our stand for freedom as in the olden time."

Winston Churchill, regarding the outcome of the Munich Crisis and the ceding of Czechoslovakia to Hitler

This map shows the main areas of European conflict during World War II. In the early years of the war, the Allies were surprised by the speed and efficiency of Hitler's war machine. Once the U.S. entered the war, however, the Allies' ships, airplanes, and tanks proved decisive.

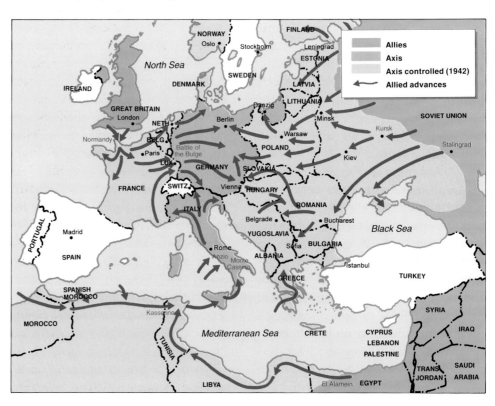

war on Germany under the terms of a treaty with Poland. In a move that hinted at what would become its territorial ambitions after World War II, the Soviet Union absorbed eastern Poland, Latvia, Estonia, Lithuania, and Finland in early 1940.

Hitler Conquers Europe

France and Britain, fighting in a piecemeal and uncoordinated fashion, had never faced anything like the German *Blitzkrieg,* or "lightning war." This military strategy of fast-moving, modernized armies using tanks and planes caught the Allies unprepared as they relied on old-fashioned permanent fortifications and trenches, some in place since World War I. In mid-1940, Denmark and Norway were quickly captured by the Nazis. By May, the British were forced out of continental Europe in the nearly disastrous retreat of 350,000 French, Belgian, and British soldiers from the beaches of Dunkirk, France, to England's shores. France surrendered on June 17. By late summer, Hitler controlled most of western Europe.

Lend-Lease

In the summer of 1940, the German *Luftwaffe* (air force) sent thousands of bombers to southern England in the hopes of softening Britain for an invasion. But Britain's Royal Air Force proved heroic, shooting down seventeen hundred enemy aircraft and blocking Hitler's planned invasion. In the course of the battle, the RAF lost more than nine hundred aircraft.

As the Battle of Britain raged in the skies over southern England, public opinion in the United States began to shift away from isolationism and toward involvement in Britain's war effort. Many Americans believed Germany would attack the United States next. Many simply felt that something had to be done to help Britain in the fight against the Nazis. Early in January 1941, Roosevelt introduced the Lend-Lease bill to Congress.

FDR had explained Lend-Lease this way in a press conference on December 17, 1940: "Suppose my neighbor's house catches fire. If he can take my garden hose and connect it up with my hydrant, I may help him put out the fire. Now what do I do? I don't say to him, 'Neighbor, my garden hose cost me fifteen dollars; you have to pay me fifteen dollars for it.' What is the transaction that goes on? I don't want fifteen dollars — I want my garden hose back after the fire is over." This simple analogy was part of FDR's brilliant strategy to get Congress to abandon isolationism, and it worked. The Lend-Lease bill granted Roosevelt powers to aid countries whose defense was deemed essential to the defense of the United States. The U.S. would lend planes, tanks, and ships to Britain, and in return Britain would lease certain military bases to the United States. This way, Roosevelt could now help his allies but had no clear mandate to declare war himself; America was not under direct attack. But war with Japan was a possibility.

Power in the Pacific was long held by the United States and its allies, who collectively had colonies in Indochina, Sumatra, Malaysia, Hong Kong, Singapore, and the Philippines. Japan wished to unseat them. Germany's invasion of continental Europe and its pressure on Britain rendered

> *"This decision [to aid Britain] is the end of any attempts at appeasement, . . . the end of compromise with tyranny and the forces of oppression."*
>
> FDR

vulnerable the Pacific colonies of European nations. Japan saw its chance and took it.

Japan had invaded China in 1931–1932 to cement its position as the main regional influence. Roosevelt supported the Chinese and placed economic sanctions on Japan. From this point onward, U.S. relations with Japan had steadily deteriorated. All through the last days of November and into early December 1941, the Japanese embassy in Washington negotiated for peace, while Roosevelt

"Air raid! Pearl Harbor! This is no drill!" Admiral Patrick N. L. Ballinger's chilling broadcast at 7:58 A.M. on the morning of December 7, 1941, was to shatter the complacency of the U.S. military. Dubbing it "a date which will live in infamy," President Roosevelt asked Congress to declare war on Japan the very next day. At the same time, Germany and Italy, as members of a triple alliance with Japan, declared war on the United States.

monitored the secret messages Japan was sending to that very same embassy. From these it was clear that the Japanese would attack very soon, but where?

Pearl Harbor

On Sunday, December 7, 1941, at 7:55 A.M. Hawaiian time, the first wave of 366 Japanese bombers attacked the warships and fighter planes at rest in the U.S. naval base at Pearl Harbor. Many Americans first thought that it was their own side conducting close maneuvers. But as the bombs began to fall and the fireballs exploded, reality set in. Pearl Harbor was caught completely by surprise. The U.S. Pacific fleet was almost wiped out in this attack. More than twenty-four hundred soldiers died, eighteen ships were sunk or badly damaged, and almost two hundred airplanes were destroyed by the Japanese.

Americans' reaction to the attack was one of shock, disbelief, horror, and then terror. Many thought the West Coast would come under attack next. But the Japanese had miscalculated. Rather than intimidating the U.S., the attack at Pearl Harbor served immediately to mobilize the country. The nation's long period of isolationism was suddenly over. America declared war.

America Mobilizes

On December 8, Congress declared war on Japan. Then, in a surprising reversal of his previous policy, Hitler declared war against the U.S. on December 11. It would prove to

be his most grievous miscalculation of the war. Germany's seven-month siege of Moscow in the bitter winter cold had cost the Nazi army over two hundred thousand men, and their target had not been captured. In full retreat by the end of December, the Germans had neither the manpower

nor the material resources to fight the United States. But Hitler was confident that the U.S. would be vanquished by Japan. What's more, with America involved in a Pacific war, its attention would not be on Europe, giving Hitler, or so he thought, total power in the Atlantic. But it was Hitler whom Roosevelt most wanted to fight, and it was upon Europe that Roosevelt turned America's attention first and foremost.

Overnight, the United States went from being a partly neutral observer to a key player on two fronts of a world war. No country had more manpower or raw materials to throw at its enemy than the United States.

Propaganda rapidly fueled intense hatred of the Japanese, but their march across the Pacific went on. Through early 1942, they forced General Douglas MacArthur out of the Philippines before turning their attention to Singapore, Borneo, and the Dutch East Indies. They were soon threatening the continent of Australia. This American poster was in response to the Japanese attack on Pearl Harbor.

"Yesterday, December 7, 1941 — a date which will live in infamy — the United States of America was suddenly and deliberately attacked by naval and air forces of the Empire of Japan . . . . No matter how long it may take us to overcome this premeditated invasion, the American people, in their righteous might, will win through to absolute victory."

President Roosevelt, War Message to Congress, December 8, 1941

And the demand for both was huge. Suddenly, everyone was joining the army. Patriotism was in style. Everyone, military and civilian alike, focused on winning the war. Britain and occupied Europe rejoiced. With the U.S. in the war at last, Hitler's rapid defeat was sure to follow.

But America's entry into the war did not guarantee victory. The enemy proved tenacious and determined. As 1942 began, Japan captured the Philippines and forced General Douglas MacArthur to retreat to the island of Corregidor. The fall of Singapore followed in February, and the Allies sustained heavy losses in men and machinery in the fierce Battle of the Java Sea. Then the Japanese made massive thrusts into Malaya, Borneo, and the Dutch East Indies.

The Japanese were brutal to their Allied prisoners of war. To be captured by the Japanese almost certainly meant death. Thousands of American, British, Australian, Canadian, and Indian POWs were routinely bayoneted to death or shot in the back of the head. Many more were forced to build roads, railways, and camps for their captors under cruel conditions that also exacted a large death toll.

The Jewish Holocaust

But atrocities were taking place elsewhere, too. Early in 1942, the first word of large-scale atrocities against European Jews reached Washington.

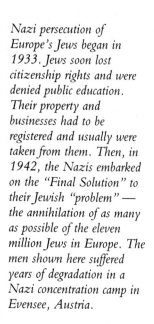

Nazi persecution of Europe's Jews began in 1933. Jews soon lost citizenship rights and were denied public education. Their property and businesses had to be registered and usually were taken from them. Then, in 1942, the Nazis embarked on the "Final Solution" to their Jewish "problem" — the annihilation of as many as possible of the eleven million Jews in Europe. The men shown here suffered years of degradation in a Nazi concentration camp in Evensee, Austria.

On January 20 at the Wannsee Conference, Hitler had ordered the "final and complete destruction of as many of Europe's eleven million Jews as possible." Hitler also targeted Communists, the mentally ill, homosexuals, priests, criminals, Russians, Ukrainians, Czechs, Gypsies, and anyone sympathizing with or caught protecting Jews.

In mid-July, Heinrich Himmler, Hitler's dreaded head of the Gestapo (secret police), ordered the "total cleansing" of Polish Jews. By the end of 1942, three million Jews had been murdered in Poland alone. The magnitude of the horror is difficult for the human mind to comprehend. Yet it continued right up until the end of the war, with increasing ferocity and desperation on Hitler's part as Germany began to lose ground. In the end, an estimated twelve million European civilians, including at least six million Jews, all perished at the whim of the Nazi tyrant.

Japanese-American Internment

President Roosevelt likewise decided on March 19, 1942, to intern Japanese-Americans in concentration camps, ostensibly to prevent spying and sabotage. (Americans of German and Italian heritage were not similarly interned, however.) Though no Japanese-American citizens were murdered, their homes were seized, their possessions confiscated, and their freedom lost. They were never formally charged with disloyalty to their country, but they were given no means to appeal their loss of property or freedom. These American citizens were deprived of their constitutional rights without due process of law. To many Americans, the Japanese-American internment, while not of the magnitude of Hitler's treatment of the Jews, was a shameful act of racism and cultural genocide in its own right. Not until 1988 did the U.S. Congress officially apologize — and make formal reparations — for the internment of Japanese-Americans, the violations of their basic civil and constitutional rights, and their loss of property and human dignity.

The Battle Escalates

In 1940, Stalin's moves into central eastern Europe had led to Nazi-Soviet bickering. Hitler wanted these

Though not nearly as horrific as German treatment of the Jews, the internment of America's Japanese population was criticized by many as inhumane, unjust, and unnecessary. By December of 1942, 110,000 Japanese-Americans, more than two-thirds of whom were born in the U.S., were locked behind barbed wire as a threat to national security. Here, a Japanese-American mother and her children are moved from Bainbridge Island, Seattle, Washington, to an internment camp in California in March 1942.

"I have never heard or read of this kind of fighting. These people refuse to surrender. The wounded will wait till men come up to examine them, and blow themselves and the other fellow to death with a hand grenade."

Major General Alexander A. Vandegrift in August 1942 about Japanese soldiers

lands for Germany, and so, breaking the terms of the Nazi-Soviet Non-aggression Pact, Hitler ordered his army to prepare an invasion of the Soviet Union, which began June 22, 1941. On January 1, 1942, the Soviets signed the Atlantic Charter with the United States, Britain, China, and France, in which it promised not to make a separate peace with Germany, now its declared enemy.

News of another proposed German campaign against the Soviet Union that spring alarmed Stalin. He pressed Roosevelt and Churchill for the opening of a second front in northern Europe to divert Germany's resources away from his borders. The United States and Britain could not yet conduct such an invasion, so Churchill offered to step up British supplies to the Russian army and to provide heavy bombing raids on Germany itself. Beginning in April and lasting through the rest of the year, Allied bombing raids on major German cities destroyed a great deal of the nation's military manufacturing capability and demoralized Germany's civilian population.

Meanwhile, in March 1942, the Japanese had captured one hundred thousand Dutch, British, Australian, and U.S. troops in Java and pressed on toward India, capturing sections of the Indian coastline. General MacArthur, nearly surrounded in the Philippines, spent thirty-five hours in Japanese-held territory, narrowly escaping from Corregidor to Australia and later proclaiming, "I came through and I shall return."

Battle in the Pacific

In May, the U.S. took part in the first air and naval battle in history, the Battle of the Coral Sea. The ships involved did not fire at one another; rather, all the fighting took place between planes launched from the ships, or between planes and enemy ships. It was a turning point in the Pacific War: The Japanese fleet lost many trained pilots and had to abandon its drive to capture Australia. In June, the United States scored another victory in the Battle of Midway Island. The U.S. Navy retook this crucial Pacific stopping place and regained its naval advantage in the region. Thus began the Allied strategy of island-hopping, which dictated the course of events in the Pacific War.

Later that summer, the U.S. launched its first offensive against the Japanese, on the island of Guadalcanal in the Solomon chain. Fierce and brutal fighting continued into 1943. To the astonishment of the victorious U.S. troops, Japanese soldiers refused to be captured, committing suicide before their captors' eyes rather than face internment.

Meanwhile, back home, the U.S. Atlantic seaboard was the scene of much naval destruction as lurking German submarines shot at easy aquatic targets lighted by U.S. coastal cities, where no blackout regulations as yet existed. In February, 65 merchant vessels were sunk in this way; in March, 273 were lost. These incidents were not widely publicized in the United States, however, for fear of panicking the population.

Germany Begins to Falter

The Allies were attaining the upper hand in Europe, though victory was by no means certain. The Germans had again attacked Stalingrad, a

A U.S. Marine, his skull-like face smeared with protective cream, operates a flamethrower during the bitter fighting for the Japanese-held island of Guadalcanal in August 1942. Once they had taken the island, the marines were amazed to see wave after wave of Japanese kamikaze attacks — suicide missions — in which the enemy often lost ten men to each marine killed.

battle that lasted well into the winter. The Russians once again stood their ground. With Germans occupying the city, the Russians refused to surrender, and eventually encircled the German army, causing Hitler to give up any hope of ever conquering the Soviet Union. By year's end, he was in full retreat.

The battle in North Africa, like the battle in Russia, was for precious natural resources, primarily gas and oil, without which Germany would lose the war. Hitler's desert troops under Field Marshall Rommel had also been in retreat since autumn. In October, the Germans suffered a decisive defeat at the hands of the British General Montgomery at El Alamein. Within three days of the American landing on the North African coast in early November, the largest amphibious

"Now this is not the end; it is not even the beginning of the end, but it is perhaps the end of the beginning."

Winston Churchill on November 9, 1942, after Allied forces pushed Rommel's forces out of El Alamein

General Dwight "Ike" Eisenhower. (1890-1969)

"I've always loved my wife. I've always loved my children. I've always loved my grand-children. I've always loved my country."   — On his deathbed, March 28, 1969

Known to his schoolmates as "Ugly Ike," Dwight David Eisenhower grew up a hard-working Kansas farm boy in a fundamentalist Christian home. An average scholar and athlete, Eisenhower had a very religious but dirt-poor childhood that he was determined to escape. Dreaming of an all-expense paid college education, Ike dodged his parents' pacifist teachings and applied for admission to the U.S. Military Academy at West Point.

The rigors of cadet life were no hardship to the work-toughened boy with six broth-ers. Though an indifferent student with a long list of demerits, Eisenhower had demon-strated leadership and good judgment in athletics, and took very solemnly the officer's code of military honor. He was commissioned into the army as a second lieutenant in the infantry upon his graduation in 1915.

In 1916, Eisenhower married Mamie Geneva Doud, and they had two sons. Not an especially charismatic offi-cer, Eisenhower rose through the ranks on the strength of confidence in his own decisions, an especially useful trait in the army bureaucracy. People were drawn to his quiet but firm leadership and his generous sense of humor.

Eisenhower was, however, a tough, career-minded soldier who had a special knack for military strategy. After unsuccessfully trying to stem the Japanese tide in the Philippines in 1941, Eisenhower became chief of the War Plans Division in 1942, formulating the invasion of western Europe as the way to defeat Hitler, defend Rus-sia, and have enough army and munitions left to fight in the Pacific. Here was the right man in the right place at the right time.

Arriving in England in June 1942, he was appointed Supreme Commander of the Allied Expeditionary Forces in Europe, largely on the strength of his invasion strategy. He had long advocated having a supreme commander who would coordinate all the various military branches for all the Allies. Difficult as this was for some high-ranking military officers to accept, it was much more efficient.

Eisenhower coordinated all the plans that led up to the D-Day invasion and supervised their execution. It took two years and all his energies to plan the invasion of Nor-mandy and gain support for his strategy from the Allies. Through all of this, he remained charming, gentlemanly, and persuasive, while he saw to everything personally, even the smallest details of the invasion.

The largest air and land invasion in military history, Operation Overlord in June 1944 completely surprised the German armies on the French coast, so beginning their great retreat. Eisenhower then orchestrated the German surrender. On V-E Day on May 7, 1945, Americans hailed him as a world hero, the architect of victory, and the greatest mil-itary strategist of his time. His return home and subsequent victory tour made him one of the most admired men in America.

Following the war, Eisenhower remained in Europe as commander of the U.S. occupation forces in Germany and was chief of staff of the U.S. Army from 1945 to 1948 as the Cold War unfolded. In the late forties, Eisenhower retreated somewhat from public view to become president of Columbia University, but he reentered public service in 1950 as Supreme Commander of the Allied forces in Europe. He resigned from the mili-tary for good in 1952 to be elected the thirty-fourth president of the United States, a posi-tion to which he was reelected in 1956.

invasion in the history of warfare until then, the Allies controlled over thirteen hundred miles of African coastline. The invasion diverted some of Hitler's resources from the Russian front and gave the Allies ground from which to attack Italy.

Dieppe

The summer of 1942 saw the Allied raid on Dieppe, France, the point of which was to practice landing techniques for an eventual counterinvasion of Europe. Though two thousand Allied troops were killed, the raid made Hitler aware of the vulnerability of his northern border, where he came to expect some sort of invasion. From the Dieppe raid, the Allies learned what Britain's First Earl Mountbatten, the supreme Allied commander in Southeast Asia, termed "the priceless secret of victory." These words alluded to the gigantic Allied invasion that was to arrive on French shores two years hence, and for which even then, American troops were training in secret in Scotland.

By the end of 1942, three decisive battles had been won by the Allies: at Stalingrad, by the Soviet Union; at El Alamein, by Britain; and in Guadalcanal, by the United States. The tide had turned for the Allies, yet the cost in lives and material had been terribly high, and Hitler still controlled most of Europe.

Glimmers of the Nuclear Age

Inklings of the impending atomic age began to surface. In April 1942, the Allies' concerns over Germany's potential to make atomic weapons centered on a German "heavy water" production plant in Vermork, Norway. (Heavy water, which has hydrogen atoms of greater than usual mass, is needed to make atomic bombs.) Operation Swallow, launched October 18, 1942, saw four Norwegian patriots parachute into Norway and organize the destruction of the heavy water plant. The plant was finally blown up on February 16, 1943, and Germany's ability to make atomic bombs was all but erased.

Signs of the Cold War also erupted in 1942. Klaus Fuchs, a German refugee and British citizen as of August 1942, was working on the atomic bomb for the Allies. Fuchs simultaneously passed atomic secrets to the Soviets. The end of World War II was not yet even in sight, but the future powers of the Cold War had begun to play their potentially deadly cat and mouse game.

On December 2, scientist Enrico Fermi produced the first nuclear chain reaction in his laboratory in Chicago. For the first time, scientists began to think that their dream of a weapon of mass destruction was possible.

NUCLEAR AGE

For further information see primary source entries on pages

11: 1565-67; **12:** 1651-52, 1666-69, 1690-92, 1698-1700

The Casablanca Conference

To capitalize on their recent victories, the Allies met in Casablanca from January 14-24, 1943, to plan the invasion of Europe. Roosevelt and Churchill were concerned that Stalin, whose forces were suffering repeated losses on their front against Germany, would still entertain the prospect of making a separate peace with Hitler. They knew that an Allied invasion of Europe would draw Hitler's resources

June 1944. Citizens of Rome greet the Allied forces as they sweep into their historic city. But, although the Italians had capitulated, the Germans refused to give up that easily. It took a combined force of Poles, Americans, British, Indians, Canadians, South Africans, Free French, and New Zealanders to rout the defending army.

away from the eastern front and thus relieve pressure on the Soviet army. This was an attractive prospect for Stalin, but unfortunately, Roosevelt and Churchill reported to the Soviet dictator that an invasion was impossible until 1944. Once the Allies did invade, however, they would not allow Germany to keep any of its territorial gains and would insist on Hitler's total and unconditional surrender. Stalin, suspicious of their motives yet desperate for aid, grudgingly agreed to wait, satisfied with the continued saturation bombing of Germany's cities.

With Germany out of North Africa and a successful Allied invasion of Sicily in July, Italy wavered in its commitment to the Axis alliance and finally signed a secret armistice with the Allies on September 3, 1943. This gave the Allies free access through Italy to the German southern flank. On October 13, Italy's new government decided to declare war on Germany, its former ally that now occupied the country.

Anzio

With Germans occupying southern Italy, the United States attempted to establish a route to Rome by landing on the beach at Anzio on January

"Full victory. . . . Nothing else," were General Dwight Eisenhower's orders to American troops going ashore in Normandy during the D-Day landings. In an operation that eventually involved eleven thousand ships, approximately three million soldiers were transported across the English Channel. At first, Hitler believed the move was a feint, and his response was slow and confused. By the time that the German dictator swung his panzers into action, the Allied beachheads had already been secured.

22, 1944. This beachhead was hard won, and the Germans gave up territory only after months of fierce fighting with heavy losses on both sides. On May 18, the Allies finally captured the monastery at Monte Cassino — a strongly held German defensive position that the Allies had not been able to penetrate. The Allies advanced rapidly on to Rome from there, liberating the ancient city on June 4.

Because of Germany's severe fuel shortages, the tide began to turn for the Allies in 1944, despite the heavy losses suffered at Anzio on the western coast of Italy. British intelligence, as it had throughout the war, continued to intercept and decode top secret messages of the German high command, enabling the Allies to anticipate almost every move the enemy made. But perhaps most significant to the war's outcome was the sheer size of the U.S. contribution, both in personnel and equipment. The United States out-produced the enemy, while

Germany's overtaxed resources dwindled.

As early as the spring of 1943, the Allies were preparing for their large-scale invasion of the European continent. This entailed top-secret training in England and Scotland; the deliberate misleading of the German army to think the invasion would occur simultaneously in Scandinavia, southern France, and Greece; and round-the-clock saturation bombing of Berlin.

D–Day: Operation Overlord

On June 6, 1944, only two days after the Americans took Rome, the largest invasion force in military history — Operation Overlord — landed on the beaches of Normandy, France. This Allied force consisted of some 4,000 ships, 600 warships, 10,000 planes, and over 175,000 troops — and it was a total surprise. Despite the Allies' massive invasion, Hitler insisted

WORLD WAR II

For further information see primary source entries on pages

11: 1556-65, 1567-70

"Salut!" Three American soldiers celebrate the ousting of the Germans at this makeshift Paris cafe in 1944. The American novelist Ernest Hemingway joined the liberators as they entered his beloved city in August 1944. The story goes that he went to visit his old friend, artist Pablo Picasso, and gave him a large box of hand grenades as a present!

that Normandy was just a diversion. He consequently continued to limit his troop movements to the west, spelling certain defeat for his army as the Allies rapidly fought their way across occupied France. Churchill proclaimed the D-Day invasion "the most difficult and complicated operation that has ever taken place."

Recapturing the Pacific

Meanwhile, the war in the Pacific was advancing well for the Allies, though the Japanese continued their policy of fighting to the last man. A January invasion of the Marshall Islands, the June 15 air raid of B-29 Flying Fortress bombers over Japan, and the offensive on the Mariana Islands of Saipan, Guam, and Tinian in mid-June 1944 — all raised the Allies' hopes that the tide had turned in the Pacific. But for the U.S. military, who had repeatedly witnessed the ferocity of Japanese soldiers in standing their ground to the last inch, it became clear that the Pacific war could drag on indefinitely, with heavy losses for the Allies.

Victory in Sight

In August 1944, aided by another huge Allied landing in the south of France, General George Patton's troops had the German army in full retreat from France. By August 25,

Paris was liberated. By October, the Allies had liberated Brussels, while the Soviets pushed westward into Hungary and Yugoslavia. The Allies, intoxicated with their steady march into formerly occupied lands, were poised on the brink of the enemy border itself.

That November, President Roosevelt, looking wan and thin from overwork, won reelection to an unprecedented fourth term by a comfortable margin of three million votes. Though a popular president, Roosevelt was not universally loved in Washington political circles. His election to a fourth term prompted Congress to pass a law preventing any president from serving more than two consecutive terms in office.

The Battle of the Bulge

Though clearly on the retreat, Hitler was determined not to give up yet. In a desperate, last-ditch attempt to recapture crucial coastal grounds, Hitler ordered his army to retake the Belgian city of Antwerp. Marshalling its dwindling supplies of fuel, machinery, and troops at the Belgian border over a period of months, the German army staged its final great counteroffensive of the war in the Ardennes Forest beginning December 16, 1944. The U.S. Army was taken completely by surprise. A quarter-million German troops, some of them posing as Americans in uniform, quickly overran the eighty thousand Allied troops near Malmedy, Belgium, and drove a forty-mile-deep bulge in the front line, completely encircling the U.S. Army at Bastogne. Thus, the attack became known as the Battle of the Bulge. Hundreds of American troops

were massacred at Malmedy, and the death toll in battle ultimately reached nineteen thousand Americans and forty thousand Germans. Hampered by dense fog, the Americans had to wait until December 23 before they could counterattack, but by December 31, the Allied air forces had reestablished air superiority over the region, and the Germans could barely make a move without fierce bombardment. When the German tanks ran out of fuel near the River Meuse, their offensive came to a standstill. They never came closer than seventy miles to their target, Antwerp.

By the end of the year, virtually all territories held by the Germans on the western front had been retaken by the Allies. On March 7, 1945, the Americans crossed the Rhine River into Germany for the first time as a conquering army.

The Meeting at Yalta

In the Crimean resort town of Yalta, the Big Three of Roosevelt, Churchill, and Stalin met in February 1945 for the last time to discuss the postwar boundaries of Europe, particularly those of Poland. FDR and Churchill were deeply worried about Stalin's tightening grip on Poland, but the Soviet dictator promised that free elections would be held there, as well as in all the countries that the Red Army occupied. Roosevelt felt confident that he had gained peace in Europe with this guarantee. Stalin, for his part, counted on America's distaste for attacking the Soviet Union as the basis for his plan to keep eastern Europe for himself.

For the United States in 1945, ending the war in Japan had taken

"There is not much comfort in looking into a future where you and the countries you dominate, plus the Communist Parties in many other States, are all drawn up on one side, and those who rally to the English-speaking nations and their associates or Dominions are on the other. It is quite obvious that their quarrel would tear the world to pieces and that all of us leading men on either side who had anything to do with that would be shamed before history."

Winston Churchill in a telegram to Josef Stalin April 29, 1945

This map shows the principal Allied advances in the Pacific. Island-hopping took a heavy toll of humans and equipment.

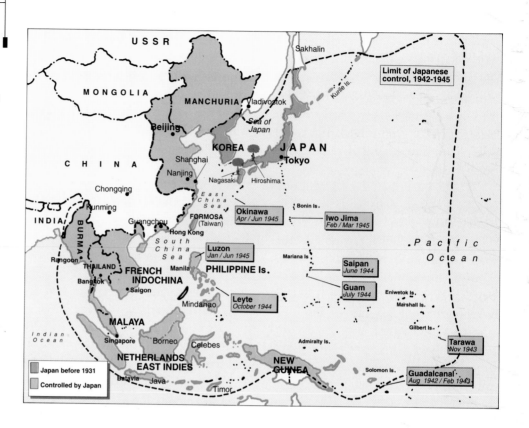

"The Japanese fought to die, and the Americans fought to live."

Witnesses of the battle on Leyte Island, where almost 80,000 Japanese soldiers died in the same battle as 3,508 Americans

priority over Europe, and it was at Yalta that Roosevelt convinced Stalin to join in the fight. Though Roosevelt had been briefed the previous September that the atomic bomb would, in all likelihood, be ready for use in August 1945 and that it would contain the explosive force of twenty thousand tons of TNT, he could not rely on this as-yet-untested weapon. An invasion of Japan was thus planned for the coming November with Soviet help. Given the tenacity of the Japanese army, Allied leaders grimly calculated that up to a million Allied personnel might die in this invasion.

In return for Stalin's aid in Japan's defeat, FDR and Churchill agreed to Stalin's demands, granting him Soviet control in Manchuria, Mongolia, and territories in the Kurile Islands off Japan, an occupation zone in Korea, and veto power in the United Nations Security Council. All of this was in addition to the territories the Red Army now occupied in eastern Europe. Many thought Roosevelt had given away the store.

The Battle for Okinawa

With the European theater of operations involved mainly in mopping up, the war in the Pacific intensified. A bitter battle on the island of Iwo Jima gave the Americans a place from which to launch air raids on Tokyo. On March 9, 1945, the single deadliest bombing raid in history resulted in 130,000 dead and sixteen square miles burned in the Japanese capital. But this was merely a prelude to the largest land battle in the Pacific war, the Battle for Okinawa, which was begun on April 1, 1945.

Okinawa Island, 360 miles to the southwest of the Japanese mainland, was the spot from which the Allies wanted to stage the November invasion of Japan. The numbers involved in the Okinawa fight stagger the imagination: 180,000 U.S. battle troops and 368,000 support personnel took part; 107,000 Japanese soldiers, 150,000 native Okinawans, and more than 13,000 Americans were killed; almost 6,000 Japanese aircraft were shot down; 34 U.S. warships were sunk in 1,999 kamikaze (suicide pilot) attacks. For eighty-two days the battle raged, until at last the Allies were victorious.

FDR Dies

In early April, the Americans stormed across Germany, liberating many concentration camps as they went, including Ohrdorf, Buchenwald, Bergen-Belsen, and Dachau. The shock and revulsion of the American troops as they met the sick and starving victims burned into the brain of many a soldier.

In the midst of all this horror, President Franklin Delano Roosevelt died of a cerebral hemorrhage on April 12, 1945, at his retreat in Warm Springs, Georgia. He had been elected four times, a feat never before accomplished in U.S. presidential politics. FDR had served his nation for twelve years, through the bitterest economic depression and the biggest war in the nation's history. Worn out and suffering from hypertension and heart disease, Roosevelt was only sixty-three when he died. He was buried at his home in Hyde Park, New York. The entire country mourned.

Stepping into Roosevelt's shoes was a man virtually unknown to America, Missourian Harry S. Truman. President Truman had, as vice president, been kept totally in the dark about the Manhattan Project, so it was a great surprise to him to learn of the atomic superweapon soon to be at his disposal. Change was also in the wind in Britain. Winston Churchill, the man who had led his country stalwartly through the darkest days of battle, had been voted out of office, to be replaced by Labour party leader Clement Attlee. Of the Big Three, only Stalin remained in power.

The Fall of Berlin

On April 16, 1945, the Soviets launched their invasion of Berlin. Despite Churchill's warning to General Dwight Eisenhower to "shake hands with the Russians as far to the east as possible," it was the Soviets who overtook the German capital first, flying the Soviet flag from the roof of the Reichstag by early May.

With mortar shells pounding his

May 2, 1945. Russian troops hoist the hammer and sickle, their national flag, over the Reichstag, or German Parliament. Hitler was presumed dead by his own hand two days earlier, and on May 7, German leaders signed an unconditional surrender. The war in Europe was over at last.

The first atomic bomb was dropped on the Japanese city of Hiroshima on August 6, 1945. President Truman then called upon the Japanese government to surrender or face a "rain of ruin" from the air. Following their refusal, he authorized the dropping of a second bomb on Nagasaki, shown here. In this explosion, 40,000 people were killed and the entire city was flattened.

bunker, Adolf Hitler sat down to write his political testimony on April 29; not surprisingly, he blamed the Jews for the war. The next day, he married Eva Braun, poisoned her, then killed himself with a single shot in the mouth. Thus ended the life of this charismatic Austrian corporal who had wrought such unspeakable horror on the world. His remains and those of Eva Braun were doused with gasoline and burned until nothing remained of the dictator many call the most evil man in history. His former collaborator in war, Benito Mus-

solini, met a less poetic end, having a few days earlier been shot by Italian partisans and hung upside down in a public square in Milan. On May 7, 1945, Germany surrendered unconditionally. The war in Europe was over. That day was V-E Day —Victory in Europe Day — and euphoria reigned.

The Bitter End

Japan, however, vowed to "prosecute the war to the bitter end" and rejected the terms of unconditional surrender suggested by the Allies during their Potsdam Conference in July 1945. President Harry Truman made the difficult and fateful decision to drop the atomic bomb. If Japan did not surrender, warned Truman, "the alternative for Japan is complete and utter destruction."

Truman told Stalin of the atomic bomb at Potsdam, not suspecting that Stalin already knew about the Manhattan Project. Naturally, Stalin did not let on, hoping to observe the strength of the superweapon for himself.

On the morning of August 6, 1945, a B-29 bomber named *Enola Gay,* converted to carry a heavier load than usual, took off from Tinian Island with a mysterious payload bearing the inscription, "Greetings to the Emperor from the men of the *Indianapolis.*" (The U.S.S. *Indianapolis* had been torpedoed on July 29, drowning 883 men, the worst single loss at sea in the U.S. Navy's history.)

Dropping its payload over the Japanese city of Hiroshima, the crew of the *Enola Gay* watched as the bomb, named Little Boy, exploded and ballooned into an enormous, mushroom-shaped cloud of fire and

DEATHS IN WORLD WAR II

MILITARY	COUNTRY	CIVILIAN
280,000	AUSTRIA	125,000
110,000	BELGIUM	90,000
350,000	GREAT BRITAIN	100,000
1,350,000	CHINA	850,000
30,000	CZECHOSLOVAKIA	250,000
200,000	FRANCE	450,000
4,750,000	GERMANY	1,470,000
400,000	HUNGARY	450,000
150,000	ITALY	70,000
1,500,000	JAPAN	500,000
6,000	NETHERLANDS	200,000
600,000	POLAND	6,000,000
340,000	ROMANIA	300,000
7,500,000	SOVIET UNION	7,500,000
408,000	UNITED STATES	2,000

Allies ▬ Axis ▬

The cost of the war in human lives was numbing.

(Below) Jubilation on Wall Street, in New York City, as the news of the Japanese surrender is announced. Celebrants clamber all over the statue of George Washington in front of the Sub-Treasury Building as thousands more stand amid the ticker tape in the business district's narrow streets.

smoke, hotter and brighter than the sun in the early morning sky. Later, it was discovered that the bomb had instantly vaporized eighty thousand people and injured thirty thousand. More than two-thirds of Hiroshima's ninety thousand buildings were utterly destroyed. Only 10 percent of the city's doctors survived, and only three of its fifty-five hospitals.

Despite this massive destruction and loss of life, no quick surrender came from the Japanese war cabinet. This indecision came at a great price. On August 9, another bomber dropped a second bomb, this one nicknamed Fat Man, over the city of Nagasaki; forty thousand more died. On August 14, the Japanese accepted the terms of unconditional surrender dictated in the Potsdam Declaration. World War II was over.

The scale of the destruction wrought by this war was beyond comprehension. Fifty million people were dead. A fearsome new weapon had been born. Warfare would never again be the same.

CHAPTER 3
On the Home Front

The Lend-Lease Act of March 1941 allowed President Roosevelt to lease or lend equipment and supplies to any nation whose defense was considered vital to U.S. security. Around 60 percent of the shipments went to Britain and its Commonwealth, in return for the lease of British-owned military bases. Here, a Lend-Lease tank comes over the side of a cargo ship in a U.S. Atlantic coast port.

Americans Spring into Action

Not only had Japan's bombing of Pearl Harbor on December 7, 1941, mobilized Americans to the war effort, it also reduced opposition to U.S. involvement in World War II to a fraction of what it had previously been. In the face of such a wholesale attack on U.S. territory, and with such massive destruction and loss of life, few Americans could object to the United States entering the war.

Despite shrinking military budgets, President Franklin D. Roosevelt had prepared as best he could for America's possible entry into the war. In 1940, he instituted the first peacetime draft in history. By the end of 1941, over 1.5 million soldiers were on active duty. Eventually, almost 32.5 million men were registered. Of these, over 15 million men volunteered or were drafted for duty. This army of unprecedented size required a heroic effort to train, feed, house, and give medical care; the techniques used to do so modernized warfare.

In addition to sheer manpower, the United States could claim its productive capability as another military asset. The nation had the resources, factories, and labor supply to out-produce the enemy. Many U.S. factories had been converted to wartime production because of Lend-Lease; the large auto makers, Chrysler, General Motors, and Ford, were already making M-3 tanks, B-25 bombers, and plane engines for sale abroad. Now they enlarged production by instituting seven-day, round-the-clock work weeks and retooled the remaining factories for war production. The enormous scale of the changeover showed in the defense budget. From 1941 to 1942, it grew from $10 billion to $52 billion. With this overnight conversion to a full war economy, the Great Depression ended.

Shipbuilding commenced on a large scale. By 1943, almost five hun-

"Pour it on." This poster exhorts Americans to maximize aircraft production. By war's end the nation had produced a staggering 85,000 tanks, 295,000 airplanes, 70,000 warships, and 5,500 merchant ships. Although the production of many peacetime commodities was either curtailed or prohibited, total industrial production of the nation practically doubled during the war years.

"There is a vast difference between keeping out of war and pretending that war is none of our business."

FDR,
third State of the Union
message

dred cargo and supply ships were set afloat each month. In 1942, FDR demanded sixty thousand planes and forty-five thousand tanks built, a seemingly impossible number. Yet, in the following year, American workers built an astounding eighty-six thousand planes. In 1944, that figure leaped to ninety-six thousand.

New materials developed for the military improved the efficiency of the nation's war machine. With some natural resources in short supply, U.S. scientists developed clever substitutes that performed better than the originals, such as plastics and synthetic rubber for metal and rubber. One billion pounds of plastics were produced for industrial uses alone. But even small things counted, such as the substitution of cellophane for tinfoil in gum wrappers, or the use of red ink instead of metal-based green. These innovations helped win the war.

Productivity came from across the social and economic spectrum of American life, not just from young white male laborers, many of whom had been drafted out of the labor force and into the military. A huge influx of women and minorities into the workforce took their place for the duration. This caused social and personal upheaval on a tremendous scale. Husbands and fathers, the traditional breadwinners of most American families, were drafted and sent overseas, and mothers, single women, and African-Americans of both sexes entered the military and paid workforce in record numbers.

Jobs sprang up in all corners of government, and new bureaucracies flourished, with such agencies as the War Production Board, Office of War Information (OWI), Office of Strategic Services (OSS), Office of Production Management, Office of Civil Defense, Office of Price Administration (OPA), and many others set up to coordinate the immense war effort.

Productivity and Privation

Most civilians threw themselves into the war effort. Unemployment almost disappeared, and by 1945, half the workforce was involved in war production. As part of the all-out effort to win the war, the War Production Board imposed unprecedented levels of control on America's economy. The agency bought $16 billion in industrial facilities and converted them to war production; it rationed millions of tons of raw materials and consumer commodities; it controlled transportation routes, labor practices, prices, and rents; and it set

production quotas in food and industry. The scale of government planning was far beyond that of World War I.

For Americans, this economy meant rising taxes, government deficits, declining investment, and growing black markets. The factory boom that produced ninety-six thousand planes in one year did not produce a similar upsurge in the standard of living, despite full employment. It did mean more people were making more money and competing for ever-shrinking supplies of goods as housing, food, and transportation grew scarce. Because of a lack of ways to spend their money, Americans saved $150 billion during the war.

Rationing

To keep supplies steady and morale even, the government imposed rationing, and for the first time, Americans lived with government-ordered shortages on a vast scale. Starting in 1943, sugar, coffee, meats, cheese, flour, fish, canned goods, and fats were strictly rationed under a system of points and ration tickets. Each family received, per week, the right to purchase four ounces of butter, four pounds of cheese, and twenty-eight ounces of meat, or their substitutes. The sale of sliced bread was banned outright. With eggs plentiful, casseroles, omelets, and souffles replaced meat, and Tuesdays and Fridays were declared meatless days. Jello often substituted for fruit. Kitchen fats were collected and exchanged for ration points. Many imported products were simply impossible to obtain, such as spices, wine, palm oil, burlap, and tea. Food rationing actually improved

"To American productivity, without which this war would have been lost."

Josef Stalin's toast at the Tehran Conference, 1943

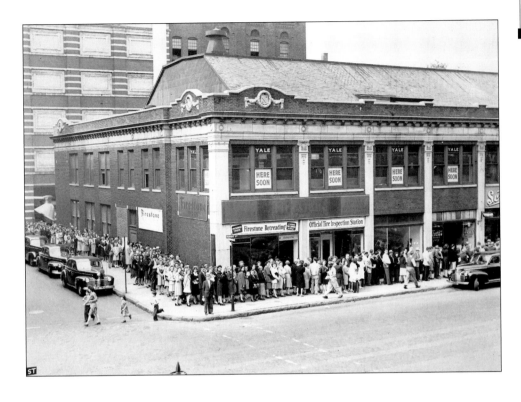

In Springfield, Massachusetts, long lines stretched around the block during rationing, which began in 1943. Each family was allowed just four ounces of butter, four pounds of cheese, and twenty-eight ounces of meat a week.

general nutrition, as limits on meats and fats led to a greater consumption of vegetables and carbohydrates.

Rationing led to other lifestyle changes. People stayed home to reduce wear and tear on their shoes, which were rationed to three pairs per year. (Sneakers ceased being made because of rubber shortages.) Strict gasoline rationing also kept folks close to home. Cars were classified as emergency vehicles and as those driven at work, those driven to work, and those driven for pleasure. Car tires and spare parts were rare commodities. A new car was unheard of: In 1942, the OPA ordered all nonmilitary car and truck production to cease completely. Paper shortages curtailed the sending of many Christmas cards, and brown grocery bags were reused. To conserve paper and shipping space, the army instituted V-mail, in which letters were photographed, developed at a reduced size, and sent

to the recipient. Though smoking hazards were as yet unknown, many quit smoking when cigarettes became scarce as tobacco land was converted to growing food crops. Of course, these were minor inconveniences compared to the severe deprivations and outright starvation of millions in Europe. In fact, most Americans felt these privations were honorable, especially in contrast to the hardships suffered during the Depression. Every effort at economy made at home meant more for the war effort and, ultimately, a quicker end to the war. A standard slogan on the home front was "Use it up, wear it out, make it do, or do without."

Farm Boom

Ironically, while Americans endured shortages, U.S. farmers produced more food than ever before.

The Depression had accustomed farmers to reducing surpluses and raising prices. Now the government exhorted farmers to produce and keep prices low. Lend-Lease increased orders to American farmers, and the rationing system allowed surpluses to go to nations that could not produce enough on their own.

To help farmers produce more, the government granted subsidies, set price ceilings to keep inflation down, and bought ever-increasing quotas of food set by the Food Requirements Committee. The government bought, on the average, half of all the butter, meats, fruits, and vegetables that were commercially produced.

Remarkably, only 5 to 10 percent of the total farming acreage was newly tilled land. Yet yields per acre increased 30 percent and outstripped food production in World War I by over 50 percent. A shift in crops and acres per crop also occurred at this time, with a 17 percent drop in cotton acreage, and a whopping 43 and 91 percent increase in oil-based crops (beans and seeds) and vegetables respectively.

Despite a labor shortage and machinery rationing (farm machinery competed with munitions for precious steel resources), farmers achieved this increase using better equipment, better crop planning, more fertilizers, better soil conservation methods, better crop strains, more effective pest and disease controls (DDT was introduced in 1942), and improved food processing and storage methods. They also benefited from unusually fair weather and imported migrant labor from Mexico and the Caribbean. Most American farmers became debt-free for the first time in decades, and their income reached an all-time high.

Labor Becomes Powerful

Labor shortages gave labor unions additional clout in calling for higher pay and better working conditions. Wages for factory workers rose a sharp 15 percent in 1942, and work weeks were extended to a mandatory forty-eight hours to meet quotas. Labor shortages caused employers to offer job perks to retain employees, such as music in the workplace, suggestion boxes, and fringe benefits that many in management saw as unnecessary frills. This feeling caused friction between management and labor unions, but the fact was that during the war, management and labor cooperated to achieve phenomenal production.

The war wrought long-term changes on the American economy. It increased federal regulation. It instituted higher income taxes. It incurred an enormous national debt. The war caused large migrations of the labor force from southern rural farms to northern manufacturing jobs. Particularly after the war, a population boom increased consumer demand, and a thriving advertising industry grew to attract the new consumers. War accelerated urbanization and the growth of suburbs, especially in the North. Wealth became concentrated in a few hundred of the wealthiest corporations (75 percent of government war contracts went to the sixteen largest corporations). Most significantly, the war caused a massive arms build-up (both nuclear and conventional). Also, following World War II, the Cold War led to an increasing proportion of the nation's economic and political resources going into the "military-industrial complex," as General Eisenhower would later call it.

Gung-ho America

Catchphrases such as "loose lips sink ships" were popular during World War II, and Hitler was a favorite target of government propaganda, which flowed in an unabated stream from the radio, movies, newspapers, magazines, and war posters — every vehicle of mass media then available. The point was clear: Each individual citizen had to do his or her bit for victory.

Everyone was gung-ho. Even famous Hollywood stars signed up for armed service. These included Gene Autry, Douglas Fairbanks, Jr., Clark Gable, Mickey Rooney, James Stewart (a major in the air force, he commanded a squadron, led eleven missions over Germany, and received

"If you talk too much, this man may die." This poster warned Americans to keep strictly to themselves any kind of information that might be useful to the enemy. The hunt was on for potential spies and saboteurs, too. On July 23, 1942, the FBI arrested twenty-eight people — including publishers and writers — and charged them with sedition. The accused, a grand jury was told, had plotted to "interfere with, impair, and influence the loyalty, morale, and discipline" of the military.

the Distinguished Flying Cross), and many others. Future president Ronald Reagan made war movies for the government, never leaving California.

On the home front, women and girls were directed to keep soldiers happy, and "accentuate the positive," in the words of a popular song. American women were told to do whatever it took to keep the fighting man

windows, with stars representing the men and women in the services.

To finance the war effort, Congress borrowed money on a grand scale, resulting in U.S. government bond sales of huge proportions. (The war would cost the United States $360 billion.) Here, too, Hollywood movie stars led bond drives for the war effort until buying war bonds

New York City schoolkids proudly display the results of their metal-saving campaign. Anything that could be recycled into armaments — newspapers, rubber, scrap metal, aluminum pots, tin cans — was collected and deposited on designated street corners. From there, students took the scrap to collection centers.

motivated and give him a symbol of beauty, youth, and freedom to fight for. The United Service Organization (USO) grew up in response to the need to build up the morale of troops stationed stateside and abroad. The USO gave war-zone concerts and tours by famous Hollywood celebrities. It also ran clubs where soldiers could meet young women with whom they could play cards, listen to the radio, dance, and drink. People hung service flags in home and shop

became synonymous with patriotism. Liberty stamps were issued with the words "for defense" near the famous statue's raised torch. Flag stamps were issued, each to honor a country occupied by the Axis powers.

Beginning in 1942, scrap drives not only became an essential component of the war economy by providing much-needed raw materials, but they helped women and children become active participants in the war effort and served as essential propa-

YOUR VICTORY GARDEN
counts more than ever!

WAR FOOD ADMINISTRATION

In 1941, Americans were exhorted by the secretary of agriculture to dig for victory, turning their back yards, vacant lots, zoos, racetracks, and even jails into vegetable gardens. These "victory gardens" eventually supplied around 40 percent of all the vegetables consumed domestically during the war.

ganda tools in getting people to support the war effort. The scrap drives were enormously successful, providing nearly half of the steel, tin, and paper for war production. In 1942, Los Angeles distinguished itself by drumming up six tons of scrap rubber tires alone. Soon, scrap metal and paper were added. That same year, the Boy Scouts salvaged 150,000 tons of wastepaper. Nylon and silk were also collected and recycled.

Food also became a way of displaying one's patriotism. People planted so-called victory gardens in their back yards or anywhere else a corner of earth presented itself. More food grown at home meant more commercial crops for the army. It is estimated that up to 40 percent of the vegetables consumed in the United States during the war were grown in victory gardens.

In 1941, neighborhood civil defense volunteers, armed with ID cards, hats, and insignia, began running air raid safety drills and enforcing blackouts and curfews. Civil defense attracted many men who were unable to serve in the armed forces because of their age or physical condition. People of all ages learned how to spot and report enemy planes and ships as part of the civil defense program.

The fashions of the time had a wartime flavor. The government regulated fabric lengths, which helped bring about a revolution in fashion, as the tight-waisted business suit (often with a military look) and pants, sensible shoes, and small hats became the standard uniform for the increasing number of working women. Fabric details were also dictated by the government. Among forbidden items were pleats, more than one patch pocket, decorative trims, hems over two-inches deep, attached hoods and shawls, cuffs, and zippers. New fabrics were developed to substitute for wool and silk, including rayon (made from wood pulp) and nylon (for stockings). With these limits, clothing separates were invented to stretch the number of outfits a woman could put together from a just few items. Women learned to make do with makeup, stocking, and hair-product shortages. Many drew lines with eyeliner up the backs of their legs in imitation of the seams of long-gone silk stockings. The result for fashion was an emphasis on simplicity, practicality, and wearability.

Censorship

Propaganda raised Allied morale and fed misinformation to the enemy. In the land of the First Amendment, another essential weapon of war — media and postal censorship — came as a shock to many at first, especially to those in the media. But so accepted was censorship as a military tool that newspapers, radio stations, and even Hollywood voluntarily adopted self-censorship codes, which gave wartime censorship a more benign and subtle nature than it had in World War I.

The military had its own censorship department, screening material relating only to military matters. On the civilian side, advertising and even domestic weather reports were heavily censored, so that troop movements and industrial outputs were kept secret from potential spies. Censorship squelched false rumors and delayed morale-damaging reports to civilians. Americans took to heart the "loose lips sink ships" reminder; self-censorship was the order of the day.

More than nine hundred censors sifted through the foreign mail in the New York post office alone, searching for illicit codes, tracking down possible spies, and deleting information that could prove helpful to the enemy, such as troop and shipping movements. By war's end, U.S. censors were spread over half the globe and numbered 14,462 people.

Spies, Crime, and Security

Censorship was only one important aspect of national security during World War II. Concerns about spying led to counterespionage tactics and beefed-up security at U.S. borders. Authorities tracked German-, Japanese-, and Italian-Americans, as well as Americans suspected of aiding the enemy. Discrimination against Americans of European or Asian descent was anything but evenhanded. For example, while Japanese-Americans were both harassed by their neighbors and sent to detention camps by the government, civilian persecution of German-Americans was actively discouraged by the FBI, supposedly because this was seen to encourage their recruitment by the enemy.

Surprisingly few attempts at enemy sabotage were made on U.S. soil. The most significant involved two boatloads of German terrorists who landed on the East Coast in the summer of 1942. But they were caught soon after their arrival.

While there was no shortage of wartime crime in the U.S. (black marketeers who sought to profit at the expense of the war effort were actively pursued and punished), violent crime rates fell. The murder rate was half of what it was during the peak of the Depression, for example, as the majority of people in the group most likely to commit homicide — young white males — were in the army. Juvenile delinquency experienced a sharp rise, a phenomenon the FBI blamed on the lack of adult supervision as more men were away, more women worked outside the home, and families moved more often, disrupting community ties.

The draft left many police departments as short staffed, as were the factories. This happened just when the need arose for extra security at the White House, foreign embassies, power plants, and other strategic sites. Auxiliary and reserves of men who had not met the military's physical requirements were used to fill in for the duration. The FBI also provided security training at defense plants.

Prior to the war, with tensions mounting in Europe and the Pacific, President Roosevelt formed the secret Office of the Coordinator of Information at the urging of William Donovan, who was a military advisor. This intelligence arm of the presidency gathered information about potential enemy countries. It was America's first civilian agency whose mission was military superiority, and its secrecy gave FDR unprecedented power. In 1942, the COI became the Office of Strategic Services (OSS), with more of a military role. After the war, the OSS became the Central Intelligence Agency (CIA), gathering information about the enemy during the Cold War.

Justice and the Supreme Court

The Supreme Court handed down several important civil rights decisions in the forties. Many felt that Roosevelt had packed the court with liberal justices. But individual liberties, overshadowed by issues of national security, came under careful scrutiny during the war, and liberal or not, the court generally sought to protect these rights.

One of the forties' most important cases was decided on June 14, 1943. The court ruled that children could not be forced to salute the flag in school if it violated their religious principles (*West Virginia State Board of Education v. Barnette*). And, in *United States v. Classic,* as a harbinger of racial issues to come, the court overruled

"With U-boats scattered throughout the Atlantic and with the possibility that German and Japanese planes might fly over American coasts, it would have been folly to permit unrestricted publication, and especially unrestricted broadcasting, of eastward-moving weather conditions."

Theodore F. Koop, deputy director of censorship

a Texas law that prevented blacks from voting in local primaries.

African-Americans Fight on Two Fronts

For African-Americans, the forties were a pivotal era, even though they are often overshadowed by the more militant and well-organized civil rights movement of the sixties. But the fact is that the civil rights movement received a terrific boost from World War II. This energy was rooted in cynicism that many blacks felt toward the war effort.

Having served in every American conflict since the Revolution but prevented from holding combat positions (except for a select few in the Civil War), African-Americans clearly saw that serving one's country had not garnered them the same rights and privileges that whites enjoyed. Also, while they contributed heavily to the war effort both at home and in the military, blacks in the forties saw little point in trying to preserve democracy abroad when it was denied them at home. This realization galvanized the movement, giving it an early focus for the fight against racial discrimination.

Early in the forties, African-Americans had just begun to get a sense of their growing political clout. Numbering thirteen million — 10 percent of the population — blacks had begun to organize trade unions, stage boycotts, hold rallies, and press for voting rights. A testament to this blossoming awareness is the remarkable growth of the National Association for the Advancement of Colored People (NAACP) during this period, from 335 chapters and 50,556 members in 1940 to 1,073 chapters and 450,000 members in 1946. During the war, the NAACP and the black press demanded that the armed forces be integrated and that all African-Americans should be eligible to apply for armed service. (Under the Army Reorganization Act of 1866, only four blacks-only army units existed. In the early forties, any African-American wanting to become a soldier had to wait for open slots in these same four units.)

Due in part to labor shortages created by white males joining the armed forces, FDR accepted more African-Americans into the army. Estimates vary widely on the number of black soldiers who served in World War II, from a low of 367,000 to a high of 700,000. It is also estimated that half of the eligible blacks served, compared with three-quarters of eligible whites. Most were rejected because of a lack of education, which was caused by discriminatory policies in schools and colleges.

While Roosevelt saw the practical benefits of encouraging African-Americans to join up, he refused to integrate the armed services, citing a potential loss of military discipline and morale. Separate facilities for the training, equipping, transporting, housing, feeding, and medical care of African-American soldiers was military law. Even blood supplies were segregated. This blatant discrimination gave impetus to the civil rights movement. The black press pointed out America's hypocrisy in using a racially segregated military to quell Germany's racist dictator, and African-Americans throughout the nation pointed out the irony of fighting a war to preserve democracy around the world when they did not share in any of the democratic rights and privileges they were trying to restore abroad.

"'Whites only,' 'whites only,' 'whites only' — I got so sick of looking at that sign that I just wanted to shoot them down."

Johnnie Stevens, member of the all-black 761st Tank Battalion in *The American Experience: Liberators: Fighting on Two Fronts in World War II*

African-Americans in the Military

The black soldier's military experience in World War II was one of extreme isolation coupled with admirable heroism. The daily reality of army life — already so regimented — under a strict policy of racial separation was a source of great stress. Separated from their white counterparts, blacks had no idea that some of the harsh treatment they received in the military was also suffered by whites; this was just army life, and it was tough.

But racially motivated indignities were commonplace as well. Black soldiers, though they wore the same uniform and fought for the same goals as their white counterparts, were more restricted in their movements around military camps than even the German POWs, and in some cases they even had to wait on POWs. Blacks had separate (and usually not equal) post exchanges, recreational facilities, and social events. Black officers were not allowed to sit with fellow white officers, but had to sit with black enlisted men. African-American army nurses were forbidden to treat white soldiers.

"I think of two armies, one black, one white. I saw German prisoners free to move around the camp, unlike black soldiers, who were restricted. The Germans walked right into the doggone places like any white American. We were wearin' the same uniform, but we were excluded."

Dempsey Travis, African-American soldier

Brigadier General Benjamin Oliver Davis, Sr., was an African-American army officer who was pulled out of retirement to supervise black fighting units during the Battle of the Bulge in 1944. His son Benjamin O. Davis, Jr., also had a distinguished military career.

Brigadier General Benjamin Oliver Davis, Jr.

Benjamin O. Davis, Jr. was the son of Brigadier General Benjamin Oliver Davis, Sr., an African-American who had served in the army since 1898 and who was pulled out of retirement to supervise black fighting units during the Battle of the Bulge in 1944. Benjamin O. Davis, Jr., had attended West Point military academy, earning top scholastic honors and becoming a fully commissioned officer in 1936. In July 1939, Davis, Sr., chose his son, Benjamin, Jr., as his aide-de-camp. The younger Davis had long wished to become a pilot but was held back by the army's refusal to train blacks as pilots.

In 1940, the army abolished this policy, and Davis took the pilot's aptitude test, scoring the second highest mark in his group. These elite African-Americans were sent to the Tuskegee Institute, Alabama, where a pilots' training school specifically for them had been set up (segregation in training, as in all else in the army, was thorough). Davis earned his wings in March 1942, was promoted to lieutenant colonel, and became a member of the first group of African-American pilots in U.S. history: the Ninety-ninth Fighter Squadron.

As the war proceeded, the Ninety-ninth was moved to North Africa in 1943. Davis was named the unit commander, the first African-American ever to command an Army Air Force combat unit. He led a 250-man crew and twenty-seven pilots in the North African, Sicilian, and Italian campaigns. He was also the first African-American to be awarded the Silver Star for gallantry in action in April 1945.

In October 1943, Davis was sent back to the U.S. to direct the training of the all-black 332nd Fighter Group, the Lonely Eagles. In January 1944, the 332nd was shipped out with its new commander. The 332nd Fighter Group became famous in military history for its splendid defense in the battle over Anzio and for the destruction of more than 250 enemy planes. For leading this effort, Davis was promoted to full colonel in May 1944 and received the Distinguished Flying Cross. The next year, the 450 pilots in the 332nd distinguished themselves again by preventing a single loss of Allied bombers to enemy planes in two hundred bombing missions during the Allied invasion of southern Germany.

After the war, Davis commanded the entire Lockbowne Army Air Force Base from 1946 through 1949. For his service during the Korean War, Benjamin O. Davis, Jr., was promoted to brigadier general. It was the first time in military history that a black brigadier general, Benjamin O. Davis, Sr., had ever pinned the stars on another black brigadier general.

Benjamin O. Davis, Jr., (on the wing) consults a fellow African-American pilot in the all-black air squadron, the Lonely Eagles, at the army air base in Tuskegee, Alabama. The Lonely Eagles flew 1,578 successful missions, receiving the Presidential Unit Citation in 1945.

These nurses, too, were forced to care only for German POWs until they protested and were finally permitted to treat any and all injured.

Black soldiers resented the military's initial refusal to use them in combat, despite their extensive training. The army commonly cited a War Department report of 1925 that said blacks were not able to learn aviation and that they made poor soldiers. Thus, most blacks found themselves in such support roles as quartermaster and stevedore.

Discrimination also extended to military justice for certain crimes committed while in the service. According to some studies, African-Americans were disproportionately punished for the same crimes committed by both blacks and whites. African-Americans made up less than 10 percent of the total armed forces. But if found guilty of murder, black soldiers were executed in four times as many cases as white soldiers who had committed the same crime. In cases in which soldiers were executed for rape, blacks made up 87 percent of the total; whites, 13 percent. After the war, African-American soldiers recalled how the army had spread vicious rumors that played to racist fears of blacks raping white women and spreading venereal diseases. In fact, blacks were strictly forbidden to fraternize with white women. For the African-American soldier patriotically doing his part for the war effort, this sort of treatment from his own army was a particularly bitter pill to swallow.

Only a few black fighting units existed, and these were primarily for show; as a rule, they were not slated for battle. These units included the 761st Tank Battalion — one of only three black armored battalions — who were the first African-Americans to fight in World War II, and the 332nd Fighter Group, the Lonely Eagles, made up of 450 elite African-American pilots who flew 1,578 missions and received the Presidential Unit Citation on March 24, 1945, for destroying 409 enemy aircraft. Some black units may also have helped liberate German concentration camps.

Black units excelled in battle, but just getting there proved to be a major hurdle. The turning point came right after the Normandy invasion and also later at the Battle of the Bulge, when shortages of white tank units finally prompted the army to deploy the black tankers. Indeed, at the Bulge, five thousand African-American soldiers answered the call for battle volunteers, so many that an African-American general, Benjamin O. Davis, Sr., was taken out of retirement in order to lead them.

Despite the segregation and discrimination, the army provided black soldiers a steady paycheck and job training that became a source of self-respect and optimism. In all, 41 percent of African-American soldiers felt the military was a positive influence in their lives (compared to 25 percent of whites). The war put many on a path leading to higher education, a greater sense of individualism, and urban living — all positive effects of military service, even though moving to the city distanced many African-American veterans from their original rural, agricultural communities.

African-Americans on the Home Front

As with whites, blacks on the home front migrated in the hundreds of thousands from the rural South to crowded northern cities, hoping to find defense plant work at higher wages. Blacks migrated at twice the rate of whites, however. What they found was much the same as whites faced: the same crowded living conditions, high rents, and shortages of food and supplies. Indeed, race riots erupted in Detroit in 1943 between whites and blacks over who would occupy public housing. But, unlike their white counterparts, African-

"If a young black fellow, eighteen years old, would get together with a British girl, sixteen, that girl would be encouraged to say she was raped. We had a number of young black soldiers who were hanged. We had one in our outfit who was hanged."

Timuel Black, African-American soldier

With the increasing demand for labor, blacks and other minorities migrated to the urban industrial regions of the North and West Coast in huge numbers. This led to the further development of urban slums like these, which lay within the shadow of the nation's capitol. It wasn't long before race riots broke out between African-Americans and whites in Detroit in the summer of 1943, and between zoot-suited Mexican-American teenagers and white sailors in Los Angeles that same year.

"We are disillusioned. We have neither faith in promises, nor a high opinion of the integrity of the American people, where race is involved. Experience has taught us that we must rely primarily upon our own efforts. . . . That is why we protest, agitate, and demand that all forms of color prejudice be blotted out."

Pittsburgh Courier, September 12, 1942

Americans also found that defense plant managers were, at least initially, unwilling to hire them. Even help-wanted ads often ran along racial lines, specifically seeking applicants who were "Nordic" or of "north European stock."

The Fair Employment Practices Commission, created by FDR in 1941, was ostensibly designed to protect African-Americans from these unfair hiring practices. But it was also designed to protect "ethnics" — that is, aliens, naturalized citizens, and even Americans of certain ethnic groups, such as Germans, Italians, and Jews — in the workplace. It was hoped that keeping these groups out of the military would prevent them from being recruited by the enemy for the much-feared but never-proven subversive body of disloyal military infiltrators called the Fifth Column. By 1943, however, when

the labor shortage became acute, plant managers who were forced to meet the huge production quotas imposed on them by the government became less picky about their hiring codes. Many blacks and so-called ethnics were finally hired in defense work, though many suffered wage discrimination.

For African-Americans, the war led to greater cohesion as they joined the growing civil rights movement following the war. Their efforts paid off when the armed forces were desegregated in July 1948 under Executive Order 9981 signed by Harry Truman. In signing the desegregation order, Truman proclaimed, "America's immediate task is to remove the last remnants of the barriers which stand between millions of our citizens and their birthrights." The civil rights movement had won its first major postwar victory.

A. (Asa) Philip Randolph. (1889-1979)

"Dear fellow negro Americans, be not dismayed in these terrible times. You possess power, great power. Our problem is to harness . . . it . . . on the broadest, daring and most gigantic scale." — June 1941.

A. Philip Randolph (he disliked his first name) was the son of a poor minister-tailor and a proud mother who taught their son a love of language through Shakespeare. The young Randolph was deeply affected by reading W. E. B. Du Bois' book, The Souls of Black Folk, which urged teaching leadership skills to one out of every ten blacks. Randolph was determined to be one of that "Talented Tenth."

After graduating from the Cookman Institute, Randolph worked on the railroad to earn enough money to go to New York City, with the dream of going to college. In New York, he enrolled at the College of the City of New York and later went on to Howard University. In 1917, with his friend Chandler Owen, Randolph established the Messenger, a militant magazine for union organizing and promoting socialism in the African-American community. In 1925, Randolph began the twelve-year fight to organize the Brotherhood of Sleeping Car Porters in an effort to improve their working conditions. In the thirties, Randolph also became president of the short-lived National Negro Congress.

When America entered World War II, Randolph worried that the war would be "the graveyard of our civil liberties." In his continuing efforts for economic equality for African-Americans (black unemployment was 25 percent in 1940), Randolph was determined to see the war plants opened to black workers. Randolph thought the way to do this was to convince African-American workers of the racial and economic discrimination against them. Thus was born the March on Washington Movement, a blacks-only activist organization, an idea widely supported by all sectors of the black community. Organizing thousands of African-Americans to come from all over the country, Randolph and Walter White, director of the NAACP, warned the federal government that African-Americans had better be allowed to work in the war plants or a mass march on Washington would take place.

A worried President Roosevelt sent his wife to dissuade Randolph, and Mayor Fiorello La Guardia tried as well, but Randolph's reply was "no earthly price can stop us." The thought of a hundred thousand African-Americans marching on Washington in the middle of an intense effort to rally the country for war led FDR to ask Randolph to the White House to try to change his mind. Randolph replied "The plants must be opened to negroes, Mr. President, or I must let my people march."

In response, the president forestalled the march by ordering war production plants to employ African-Americans, and he set up the Fair Employment Practices Commission. Randolph called off the march and the March on Washington Movement was employed in monitoring the FEPC.

In 1947, Randolph formed, with Grant Reynolds, the League for Nonviolent Civil Disobedience Against Military Segregation. Though he did not endear himself to President Truman by claiming the moral high ground in his battle to desegregate the army, Randolph's argument ultimately held sway when Truman finally ordered the army to be desegregated in 1948.

"Everyone stops to admire the scene. Rosie at work on the B-19. She's never twittery, nervous or jittery, Rosie, Rosie the Riveter. What if she's smeared full of oil and grease, Doing her bit for the old lend lease, She keeps the gang around, they love to hang around, Rosie, Rosie, Rosie, the Riveter."

"Rosie the Riveter" song

Rosie the Riveter and Her Sisters

When war broke out, white, middle-class American women did their bit for victory in traditional ways: running scrap drives, rolling bandages for the Red Cross, working in USO snack bars, selling war bonds, growing victory gardens, running a thrifty home, and taking responsibility for families with husbands away. A woman's sphere was her home and family; getting actively involved in the war itself did not yet appear to be an option.

To reinforce this role, the popu-lar press exalted the image of the stereotypical housewife as the single most important person keeping the home front happy and secure for the

"Rosie the Riveter," from the May 29, 1943, cover of the Saturday Evening Post, *painted by Norman Rockwell, was a far cry from the prewar stereotypical housewife and mother. Women began doing jobs they would never have thought of before, not just as riveters, but also as welders and mechanics. Despite initial resentment from their male coworkers, women proved equally able and efficient at all manner of industrial tasks previously denied to them.*

WORLD WAR II

For further information see primary source entries on pages

11: 1556-65, 1567-70

men to return to. The housewife of the 1940s was a popular icon representing home, freedom, contentment, and happiness. Most important, she stood by her man.

By the end of 1942, all available men were in the labor force, yet industry needed more workers. The War Manpower Commission realized that women were the largest under-employed segment of society and that bringing them into the workplace was the only way to solve the labor shortage. Assuming that women were unwilling to work, the government worried about how to convince housewives to perform industrial jobs that were essential to the war effort. The solution was a masterpiece of public relations that generated lasting images associated with the forties — most notably, Rosie the Riveter.

To sell housewives on the war, the commission teamed up with the Office of War Information (OWI) to mount a media blitz on American women to take defense jobs and join the armed forces. This campaign was not aimed at women already in the workforce, though in 1941 they made up 29 percent of the total labor force. These women, who might naturally be attracted by higher pay and higher status in the new defense jobs, were ignored by the media.

The advertising campaign undertaken by the government in 1943 retained the essentially housewifely nature of the ideal American woman of the time and repackaged her as a loyal, patriotic woman willing to serve her country by working to help end the war sooner and bring home her man. When the war was over, the campaign endlessly repeated, women would willingly retreat from their jobs back into the home, mak-

ing way for the returning soldiers. Higher wages, new job skills, and new independence were benefits downplayed by the government campaigns. The theme of service to one's country was similar to service to the family. These propaganda programs were carefully calibrated to change the image of war work into a feminine duty, as easy to perform as housework. To create this new image, government reclassified the percentage of jobs suitable for women from 29 to 55 percent. The objective was to make jobs appeal to what the government considered to be a woman's femininity. It worked. By the end of 1943, almost the entire supply of single women had been absorbed into the workforce, so the government liberalized employment laws to include married women as well.

The biggest single obstacle for women with children was child care. Only forty-three federally funded daycare centers were set up, far fewer than met the need. In 1944, 16 percent of mothers working in war jobs reported that they had no child care at all. Unlike the British government, U.S. companies did not try to accommodate a working mother's schedule by offering extended shopping hours or time off for family demands. As a result, mothers were absent from work 50 percent more often than men as they juggled babysitters, families, night shifts, and housework along with their jobs, and without their husbands' help. A rare exception was the Boeing Company in Seattle, Washington. To attract more women to join its workforce, Boeing offered round-the-clock daycare, nursing care, and nutritionists on hand to advise working mothers and their children.

"In the next twelve months, the American housewife must show that she can keep her head and her temper and roll up her sleeves at one and the same time. If she can't her menfolk fighting on distant atolls are likely to get slaughtered in the hot sun for lack of ammunition."

J. C. Furnas, "Womanpower," *Ladies Home Journal,* November 1942

Eleanor Roosevelt. (1884-1962)

Eleanor Roosevelt redefined first ladyship. Flouting tradition, she became a much-published journalist-author, civil rights activist, and vocal politician in her own right, quite apart from her official duties as presidential helpmate. As such, she set the standard for all the first ladies who followed her, and became a role model for American women in general.

Eleanor endured a lonely childhood, ignored by her beautiful socialite mother and troubled by her alcoholic father. Her parents died when Eleanor was young, and she was raised by her strict grandmother. She did not begin to discover herself until the age of fifteen, when she attended the Allenswood School near London. With the encouragement of the headmistress, she became a school leader, finally getting the attention and approval she craved from those around her.

Becoming the wife of Franklin D. Roosevelt (her fifth cousin) in 1905, she bore six children in eleven years and raised them under the domineering guidance of her mother-in-law. As Eleanor and Franklin were wealthy and privileged, Eleanor performed the social duties associated with being the wife of a U.S. senator, assistant secretary of the navy, and New York governor. But she also, during the twenties, involved herself in many activist organizations. When FDR contracted polio in 1921, Eleanor took it upon herself to keep up his interest in politics by joining political organizations and reporting back to him on their activities.

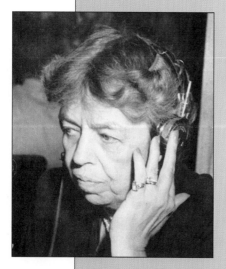

Upon becoming first lady in 1933, Eleanor Roosevelt threw herself into the job with gusto. In fact, she became something of a publicity hound, breaking precedent by holding her own news conferences, by giving lectures and broadcasts, and by traveling around the country. Her weekly "My Day" newspaper column on politics, the war, and civil rights — in which she often expressed opinions that differed quite significantly from public positions taken by her husband — was widely read. Eleanor also appeared regularly on radio programs throughout the thirties and forties.

Though by 1939 she had a popularity rating nine-points higher than her husband's, Eleanor was viciously attacked for her outspokenness. Many felt she should keep quiet and stop meddling in government business. Others admired her as a role model for women. But whatever else one felt about her she was the most controversial and publicly committed first lady in United States history.

Widow Eleanor Roosevelt taking part in a two-way broadcast from New York to Leskand, Sweden, in 1945. She and noted scientist Dr. Lise Meitner, who helped develop the atomic bomb, discuss the responsibility of women to see that atomic power be used wisely after the war.

Throughout World War II, Eleanor visited U.S. troops in Britain, the South Pacific, the Caribbean, and on U.S. military bases. In 1941, she became codirector of the Office of Civilian Defense, resigning shortly thereafter because of criticism of some of her appointments. When her husband died in office in 1945, she told reporters that "the story was over" and spent most of the rest of the year in seclusion. But by December 1945, she was back in action and was appointed a member of the U.S. delegation to the United Nations by Harry Truman. As chair of the UN Commission on Human Rights, a position she held until 1952, she was instrumental in drafting the UN Declaration of Human Rights. In 1947, she was part of the stellar group that formed Americans for Democratic Action, an organization that combined liberal reformism in domestic policy with staunch anticommunism.

Eleanor Roosevelt lived a life of committed public service and journalistic excellence. Overcoming the painful shyness, insecurity, and inadequacy she felt as a child, she had triumphed in a varied, rich, and long career as an invaluable aide to the president, as well as in carving out her own sphere. "No matter how plain a woman may be if truth and loyalty are stamped upon her face all will be attracted to her," she once wrote at the age of only fourteen.

Money, but Little Power

Women benefited in two major respects from their entrance into defense jobs: They were generally well trained and well paid. Initially, factory bosses hesitated to train the incoming women because they were viewed as merely temporary. But eventually women were indeed trained in all sorts of technical and skilled labor, to the resounding praise of their bosses, who met the government quotas of arms production because of the work of these women. For women, it was a heady new accomplishment to build a ship or an airplane or fuse a bomb. It certainly was more interesting than the boring, solitary repetitiveness of day to day housework.

A female worker's pay scale was, in many cases, equal to a man's for the same job. This was not accidental. Factories had, in fact, tried to lower the wages paid to women, but the labor unions fought back on their behalf, not to help the women, but because they wanted to prevent women from later taking these jobs from men at the lower pay rate. No factory boss, they argued, would want to rehire a man at a higher wage if he could keep a woman for less money. Thus, the first real equal pay battles were fought by labor unions during World War II. This advocacy was repaid by the women, who boosted union membership during the war. In 1940, women unionists numbered eight hundred thousand. By 1944, that number had grown to an incredible three million.

Despite the traditional underpinnings, government propaganda did create a completely new image of the American woman in the popular press: She was now a working woman. She wore overalls, sported a welding torch, and carried a lunch box. The famous cover of the *Saturday Evening Post*, featuring Norman Rockwell's Rosie the Riveter on May 29, 1943, instantly spoke what no number of slogans could say. Rosie was capable and tough, yet cheerful, well groomed, and all-American. Images like Rosie's spewed forth from Hollywood in the form of womanpower campaign films such as *The Glamour Girls of 1943,* onto magazine and pulp fiction covers, and into popular songs such as "Swing Shift Maisie," "Rosie the Riveter," "The Lady at Lockheed," and "We're the Janes Who Make the Planes." Billboards, posters, even underwear displays in department stores touted the theme of the working woman.

The new American woman was, however, still all woman, the campaign was careful to stress. Rosie and her sisters weren't really new. Beneath the blue denim and grease was the same pretty little blonde gal who made sure she kept her figure for her man, should he ever return.

Women in the Armed Services

The armed services also went to great lengths to soften the masculine image of military service in order to raise recruitment levels. The OWI touted the armed services as an excellent place to meet men, wear designer uniforms, and learn poise and self-confidence. This appeal to traditional feminine attitudes was echoed in numerous guides published to recruit American women into the services.

"Keeping the offensive surging forward is the responsibility of every American woman. . . .

This is a war of survival. This is a war which recognizes no distinctions between men and women. This is YOUR war. Will you accept the challenge?"

WAAC director
Oveta Culp Hobby

"WAACS and WAVES and women welders. . . . Where is it all going to end? . . . Is it hard to foresee, after the boys come marching home and they marry these emancipated young women, who is going to tend the babies in the next generation?"

Minneapolis Tribune,
August 25, 1942

In the middle of 1942, Congress created the Women's Army Auxiliary Corps (WAACs) and the Women Accepted for Voluntary Emergency Service, Navy (WAVES). Both units were intended for non-combatant duties at home and overseas. Their formation was not without controversy, however. Some women physicians refused to serve with the WAACs because they had been denied access to the all-male Medical Reserve Corps.

Looks and appearance were of paramount importance. Details of uniforms, weight and height limits, as well as practical items such as education and job experience, were all outlined in these guides.

One guide, *American Women in Uniform,* by Mary Steele Ross, advised recruits: "hitch your stomach to your backbone . . . you don't flit, glide or hover now you're in uniform . . . put your diamonds on dry ice for the duration . . . tresses must never touch your collar . . . never use them for a backdrop . . . be cheerful even if it maims you . . . no cherry-red nails, no red rosebud lips, but remember beauty's your duty."

In May 1942, Congress autho-

rized the creation of the Women's Army Auxiliary Corps (WAACs). President Roosevelt immediately requested a force of 25,000 WAACs, as the women were called, with an ultimate goal of enlisting 150,000. The purpose of the corps, as the president said, was "to provide women for non-combatant service with the army for national defense when needed, . . . thus enabling the release of able-bodied men in the Army from non-combatant duty to active service in combat."

Soon after came the WAVES (Women Accepted for Volunteer Emergency Service, Navy), the SPARs ("Semper Paratus — Always Ready," Coast Guard Reserve), the

Colonel Oveta Culp Hobby. (1905-1995)

"You have taken off silk and put on khaki. You have a debt to democracy and a date with destiny. . . . You are no longer individuals. You wear the uniform of the United States. Respect that uniform. . . . You are the example of free women defending a free way of life, to the exclusion of everything else, until the war against the Axis is won."
— Speech to the first class of WAAC officer candidates

As head of the Women's Army Auxiliary Corps, Hobby had the huge job of organizing, directing, and commanding the army's first all-female corps in history. She devised the structure of female non-combatant service in the army, with the mission of training women to take men's jobs, thereby freeing them for combat.

Hobby was more than equal to the task. Chosen for the job because of her exceptional organization and planning skills, she was a woman of broad executive talents. These abilities had been honed ever since her childhood in Texas. Hobby grew up in a political household. Her father, I. W. Culp, was a member of the state legislature, and she often went to work with him as a girl, asking questions of everyone she met.

Her interest in law increased as she attended Baylor College and University of Texas Law School. Later she became parliamentarian of the Texas state legislature and wrote a textbook on parliamentary law entitled Mr. Chairman.

Oveta Culp married former governor William Pettus Hobby in 1931 and had two children. But motherhood did not stop her from having a career. She worked for the Houston Post for seven years and was finally promoted to the position of executive vice president in 1938.

She kept alive her political interests by attending the National Democratic Convention in 1928, and served as secretary and parliamentarian at many state conventions. In addition, she sat on dozens of philanthropic and social boards and committees. Hobby's interests were demonstrably wide-ranging and her energy was enormous. For a woman of her time to have accomplished all this was indeed an exceptional feat.

As director of the WAACs, Hobby became one of the most photographed women in the United States. Her poise was legendary, her looks smart and sophisticated. Her colleagues credited her with "thinking like a man." She was intelligent, deliberate, orderly, and circumspect. But Hobby brought something more than just executive ability to her job. She had a deep loyalty to her country, an unselfish dedication that she expected, in turn, of her recruits.

Since one of her main jobs was to recruit 150,000 volunteer women to the WAACs, Hobby actively took part in recruitment efforts, personifying the ideal World War II military woman in her crisp uniform and with her patriotic speeches. In this she was aware of the WAACs' pioneering role in military history, and of her own as its leader and chief role model. She confronted numerous challenges for the military that resulted from the influx of so many women (though subjects such as birth control were diligently avoided).

She remained as director of the WAACs throughout the forties and became secretary of Housing, Education, and Welfare under President Eisenhower in 1953. Hobby had a sustained and effective career in her nation's service, truly remarkable in the years before the women's movement and anti-sex discrimination laws opened new career paths to women.

WOMEN'S RIGHTS

For further information see primary source entries on pages

11: 1480, 1508-09, 1521-22; **12:** 1713-14, 1717-19

Marines, and many lesser-known groups such as the WAFS (Women's Auxiliary Ferrying Squadron), WOW (Women Ordnance Workers), WIRES (Women in Radio and Electrical Service), ANC (Army Nurse Corps), WASPs (Women's Airforce Service Pilots), and so on. Ross's guide to the services lists some twenty-seven military and paramilitary organizations for women, each sporting its own uniforms, insignia, and ranks. In all, 350,000 women served in the armed forces, 140,000 of them as WAACs and an additional 100,000 as WAVES.

As volunteers, women differed greatly from their male draftee counterparts. Servicewomen could be married, but women with children were not admitted. According to at least one survey, army women were better educated than men in equivalent positions, and more came from families where one parent was a professional, while many more men came from low-income families. More than one-third of the women came from farms, two-thirds were Protestant, and less than one-third were Catholic. A very small percentage was Jewish. Fully 80 percent of the women remained single during their war service. Of the married women, only one-third had married after entering the service. Women in the services were exceptionally well educated for the time, with only 6 percent never having finished high school, as opposed to 42 percent of their civilian counterparts.

Army nurses were exceptional even within this exceptional group of women, as they required more years of training, and more than half had worked in their profession before entering the military. The nursing profession supported the highest rate of military service of any group, male or female, with almost half of the eligible civilian nurses joining the force. Nurses in the army soon discovered that they were at the cutting edge of medical practice, employing new treatments such as antibiotics to fight infection and plasma to replace excessive blood loss.

Life for women in the service was as rigorous and regimented as it was for the men, though women were not trained for combat. They had to undergo basic training, field maneuvers, military base life, and the monotony of waiting for field assignments. Women were not posted overseas until late 1943. Yet again, women's experience differed remarkably from men's. For women, and particularly for nurses, the service was an opportunity to really use their skills, to try something new, to travel, and to see the world. Almost all female veterans surveyed listed their military experience as one of the most important of their lives. For these women, the service was something unique and new, while for men it was simply what was expected of them so it had less importance.

In Their Place

As the image of the new ideal woman flooded the country, many men worried that women would become too masculine and refuse to give up their factory jobs to returning veterans. This fear contained a germ of truth, as 79 percent of working women felt that working was more fun than staying at home, according to one survey. Half of them expressed a desire to keep their

> "Even more than men, these women have become unsuited to their former civilian environment because the change in their pattern of life was more radical. . . . Most of them have matured, have broader interests and a new and finer sense of values."
>
> Army psychiatric report on veteran nurses

jobs, yet most of these same women willingly gave up their employment at the war's end to get married and have children.

One reason was that men's attitudes toward women working (and women's attitudes as well) really hadn't changed. Soldiers, though they might come into contact with field-toughened army nurses or pilots, pinned glossy photos of screen stars such as Betty Grable over their bunks and dreamed of returning to their sweethearts at home, settling down, and raising a family. A *Ladies Home Journal* survey of the soldiers' dream girl in 1942 declared a woman's cooking ability to be more important than her brains, her figure more important than her face, and her devotion to home and children more important than working in an office or factory outside the home after marriage.

Thus, while the forties may at first glance have seemed like a liberating time for women, it was so only in the popular image of women portrayed in the media. Even then, a woman's traditional role was constantly stressed, as her wartime efforts were seen as motivated by patriotism, not personal pride or gain. The feminist movement, so vigorous during World War I, stalled during World War II, with the notable exception of those advances that were made by women in labor. Even in that case, the strides made by women were done so out of concern for the role of *men* in labor, not out of women's self interest. While the feminist movement during World War I had led to woman suffrage in 1920, it reaped no similar long-term reward for working women during World War II. Rather, the message that most women received after the war was to return to their traditional roles at home, to resume their maternal position within the family, and most women complied. In fact, it was a time of terrific conformity for men and women alike, a time to put personal ambitions aside, and in doing so, women's latent political power remained hidden for another twenty or more years.

The wartime look. The sales of women's pants in 1942 were five times greater than in the preceding year. Slacks were more practical for the working woman, especially for those employed in factories. Businessmen, meanwhile, did without vests and their "victory pants" lacked cuffs.

CHAPTER 4
Dawn of the Atomic Age and the Cold War

The Manhattan Project

Harry Truman had been vice president for only five months when Roosevelt died on April 12, 1945. He knew nothing of the Manhattan Project. Prior to the vice presidency, Truman had been just a peppery and blunt but obscure senator from Missouri. As a national political figure, he was unknown, having only just replaced Henry Wallace, an ultraliberal, as FDR's running mate in 1944. Certainly, he was unloved (he received one of the lowest popularity ratings in presidential history), for the nation mourned the much-elected FDR and worried about whether the unproven Truman could lead America at a crucial moment in its history.

Truman became president on April 12, 1945, as the war with Japan dragged on, and relations with the Soviet Union were also growing tense over the balance of power in postwar Europe. Days after Truman's inauguration, he was told of the atomic bomb and its development under the direction of physicist J. Robert Oppenheimer.

Truman was surprised at the expected power of the bomb and the years of secrecy surrounding such a huge government project. The Manhattan Project had one hundred thousand people building two uranium processing plants, conducting research, and manufacturing bombs,

all at a cost of two billion dollars. Truman was further surprised to learn that the first bomb was almost ready for testing and that it promised to yield the destructive power of twenty thousand tons of TNT.

Uncertain that the bomb would work, Truman planned the Japanese invasion for November to finish the war once and for all. Military advisors predicted a million casualties. Truman wondered what such a death toll would do to American morale, but he appeared to have no alternative.

"The Gadget"

As Truman conferred in Potsdam on July 16, 1945, the first atomic bomb was detonated in an above-ground test in the desert of Alamogordo, New Mexico. The bomb, code-named Trinity, was called "the gadget" by the scientists who had created it. The gadget got its power from splitting the nuclei of uranium 235 atoms by bombarding them with neutrons. The energy released by this splitting, or fission, was one hundred times more powerful than any chemical reaction. Neutrons released by fission would, in turn, split more uranium atoms, causing a chain reaction that released power exponentially until the entire mass of uranium heated up, liquefied, vaporized, and then exploded. No one predicted the full and deadly power of this new weapon.

Dr. J. Robert Oppenheimer. (1904-1967)

"I have blood on my hands." March 1946

During the twenties and thirties, American physicist Julius Robert Oppenheimer became a world leader in theoretical physics. The son of a well-to-do textile importer, Oppenheimer graduated from Harvard in 1925 and received his Ph.D. from the University of Gottingen, Germany, two years later. In the late thirties, Oppenheimer wrote the first paper theorizing the existence of black holes in the universe.

In 1939, with many research fellowships and academic positions to his credit, Oppenheimer was named director of the Manhattan Project, the U.S. government's effort to build an atomic weapon. Under Oppenheimer's guidance, the Trinity bomb was built and tested at Alamogordo, New Mexico.

The bomb's success had a paradoxical result for its inventors, who came to dread the terrible power they had let loose on the world. Led by Oppenheimer himself, the Association of Los Alamos Scientists (ALAS) was formed in August 1945 and lobbied for control of the weapon, advocating that the U.S. share the bomb with the rest of the world to prevent anyone from having arms superiority. By 1947, the movement had several thousand members, though it never achieved its aims. Despite Oppenheimer's feelings of guilt over his role in the bomb's creation, ironically, his reputation in this field was only enhanced by the bomb.

After the war, Oppenheimer directed the Institute for Advanced Study at Princeton (where Albert Einstein had also worked), until his death from cancer in 1967. During his tenure there, he was awarded the Medal for Merit by President Truman in 1946 and continued to advise the government on nuclear issues. As a member of the Lilienthal Committee, for example, Oppenheimer devised a plan that became the core of U.S. policy regarding international control of nuclear energy. As chairman of the General Advisory Committee of Atomic Energy from 1946 to 1952, Oppenheimer helped develop further military capabilities for nuclear energy, including urging the government to develop the powerful hydrogen bomb.

After a career of distinguished service to his country, and having unleashed the atom's lethal power on the world, Oppenheimer was investigated by the House Un-American Activities Committee (HUAC). He was also put under close surveillance by the FBI for what he admitted were Communist activities in high school and college, but for which he offered no apology, saying simply, "Most of what I believed then, now seems complete nonsense, but it was an essential part of becoming a whole man. If it hadn't been for this late but indispensable education, I couldn't have done the job at Los Alamos."

To the HUAC he argued for the bomb's use only against military, not civilian, targets. The threat of bombing military targets alone, he said, would achieve America's goal of keeping the Soviets out of western Europe. Even if nuclear bombs were used against Soviet cities, Russians could still invade western Europe. The army largely supported this view, as tactical nuclear weapons enlarged its power. But these statements only fueled the HUAC's accusations of procommunist sympathies, and it revoked Oppenheimer's security clearance. Not until 1963 did the government redress this slight when President Kennedy awarded Oppenheimer the Fermi Award, but his security clearance was never fully restored.

Dr. J. Robert Oppenheimer (left), director of the Los Alamos Bomb Project, and Major General Leslie R. Groves, chief of the Manhattan Engineering District in which the first atomic bomb was developed. They are inspecting the base of the steel tower from which the first atomic bomb hung prior to testing near Alamogordo, New Mexico, in July 1944.

"To quell the Japanese resistance man by man and conquer the country yard by yard might well require the loss of a million American lives and half that number of British. . . . Now all this nightmare picture had vanished. In its place was the vision — fair and bright indeed it seemed — of the end of the whole war in one or two violent shocks. I thought . . . how the Japanese people . . . might find in the apparition of this almost supernatural weapon an excuse which would save their honour and release them from their obligation of being killed to the last fighting man."

Winston Churchill after the testing of the atom bomb at Alamogordo, New Mexico

The moment Trinity exploded, the temperature at the bomb site was three times hotter than the sun's interior. The one hundred-foot-tall steel scaffold holding the bomb vaporized. The desert sand at the bomb site melted and became glass. The resulting fireball was thirty-five thousand feet high and produced a fire storm that killed all plant and animal life within a one-mile radius. Windows blew out as far as two hundred miles away. People reported the sun rising and setting suddenly. Measurement equipment near the bomb site was demolished. Within milliseconds, enough energy had been released by the explosion to supply power to the entire nation for half a minute. As soon as the smoke cleared, scientists went to ground zero, not yet knowing the dangers of radiation, to find a crater one quarter-mile in diameter.

The test was an awesome success. A single bomb had done the work of untold squadrons of planes, tanks, and ships. Suddenly, the prospect of a so-called clean war presented itself. American troops could be replaced by this weapon. A jubilant Secretary of War Henry Stimson notified Truman that "results already exceed expectations." Truman was delighted. America's gamble had paid off.

Choosing the Target

Since 1939, it had long been assumed that if a bomb could be developed, it would be used against the Nazis. The fear that the Germans might beat the Allies to the bomb spurred its rapid pace of development. But the evidence showed the Nazis were far behind. The pace of Nazi research into atomic bomb develop-

ment could not have been the only reason for its sudden acceleration by the United States.

Targets were discussed as early as March, 1943, by the Joint Chiefs of Staff. Early in the bomb's development, it was regarded as a strategic weapon as well as a tactical one. That is, it could be used against civilian targets as well as small, mobile military ones. This strategic concept, called total war, rose out of Hitler's *Blitzkrieg,* in which civilian populations were included in military targeting. Total war using the bomb was a great psychological weapon because it could threaten entire cities in one blow. (Total nuclear war became, in fact, the heart of Cold War doctrine. Armed troops and territorial battles were seen as almost obsolete.)

With Germany defeated by the time of the Trinity test and the war with Japan grinding on, the question of how to use the new superweapon changed. Trinity made the U.S. militarily invincible. This led Truman, on July 24, to inform Stalin at Potsdam of the Alamogordo test, perhaps hoping that its destructive capacity would prevent Stalin from spreading communism throughout Europe. (Truman did not realize that Stalin already knew of the bomb and that the Soviets were working on their own version.) Thus, before it had even been deployed, the atomic bomb had been linked to the impending Cold War, to be used as a diplomatic tool rather than merely as a military weapon.

Truman noted in his diary in July, that "the Japs are savages, ruthless, merciless and fanatic." For him, Japan had become the likely target. At first, Truman suggested a demonstration of the bomb for the Japanese, but was advised that the U.S. would look

Hiroshima, Japan, after the bomb was dropped on August 6, 1945. Around 88 percent of the people within 1,500 feet of the blast died instantly. The temperature at the center of the blast reached 5,432° F. The intention of dropping the bomb was to save Allied lives, but the explosion, together with a similar blast three days later over Nagasaki, killed over 120,000 Japanese men, women, and children.

foolish if the test failed. His choice came down to the invasion of Japan or the hope that atomic bombing would force Japan to surrender. Truman pressed the Japanese with an ultimatum, on July 26, 1945. Surrender unconditionally, he demanded, or face "complete and utter destruction."

Despite growing American-Soviet tensions, Stalin agreed to demand a total surrender and promised to declare war on Japan if it did not give up. This, the Allies felt, was necessary to avoid a situation like the one created by the Versailles treaty, in which the terms of peace were dictated by outside countries, creating the German resentment that gave rise to Hitler. The Allies insisted on Japan's choosing to surrender so that the Japanese could blame no one but themselves for their defeat. Also, Stalin may have hoped that a Japanese surrender would give the USSR greater influence in the Pacific. At any

rate, the Japanese chose to ignore Truman's ultimatum.

Fearing huge troop losses in an invasion, Truman made the fateful decision to bomb Hiroshima. The target, the American public was later told, was a war industry center — though it also happened to contain three hundred thousand civilians. The bomb dropped on August 6, 1945, killing eighty thousand people instantly in a combination of the blast, the firestorm, and the thermal and nuclear radiation it unleashed.

Truman waited tensely for the Japanese surrender, yet none was forthcoming. Despite the awful devastation, Japan resolved to keep fighting. On August 9, the second bomb fell over Nagasaki. Instantly, another forty thousand were killed and the city leveled. Stalin kept his promise and declared war on Japan on August 8, 1945. The Red Army immediately invaded Japanese-held territory in

NUCLEAR AGE

For further information see primary source entries on pages

11: 1565-67; **12:** 1651-52, 1666-69, 1690-92, 1698-1700

> *"The weapon is to be used against Japan between now and August 10th. [I have instructed Henry Stimson] to use it so that military objectives and soldiers and sailors are the target and not women and children. Even if the Japs are savages, ruthless, merciless and fanatic, we as the leader of the world for the common welfare cannot drop this terrible bomb on the old capital or the new."*
>
> President Truman
> in his diary,
> July 24, 1945

Manchuria, China, and on the Kurile and Sakhalin Islands. An Allied invasion loomed. All this combined to bring about Japan's surrender on August 14.

The surrender relieved American servicemen who, with the carnage at Iwo Jima and Okinawa, were not eager to invade the Japanese mainland. Truman said the bomb had saved American and even Japanese lives by making an invasion unnecessary. Given the events at Pearl Harbor and Japanese treatment of POWs, as well as being kept in the dark about radiation and the devastation of Hiroshima and Nagasaki, most Americans felt the atomic bomb's use to be totally justified.

Potsdam Conference

Meanwhile, the Potsdam conference of July 1945 was a pivotal moment in the developing Cold War. At Potsdam, in Germany, Stalin, Truman, and British Prime Minister Attlee discussed the thorny question of Poland's postwar boundaries and its system of government. Stalin stubbornly refused to back out of lands occupied by the Red Army and to abide by his agreements at Yalta allowing self-government in Poland. Stalin had also increased the tension by initially blocking his western allies from occupying agreed-upon zones in Austria.

By August 2, the eastern half of Germany, including half of Berlin, was ceded to Soviet control since it was obvious the Russians had no intention of leaving without a fight. Plus, a ground war with Russia was out of the question. With the war in the Pacific, it was unlikely that Amer-

icans would support a new war against an ally of proven military strength, size, and endurance and for territory that the U.S. could not rightfully claim as theirs.

Truman saw that Stalin's territorial goals, whether for Russian national security or, as Truman suspected, to advance communism into Europe, would drastically alter the balance of power in postwar Europe. The idea of such a vast expanse of Communist-controlled territory made Truman and western Europe suspicious of Communist motives at best; at worst, it made them paranoid of Communist plots to take over the world. To rein in the Communist expansion, Truman relied on U.S. military might in his hopes for a diplomatic solution: He began a nuclear buildup.

The Bomb in a Cold War World

Crucial in the development of the Cold War was the fact that in the period just after World War II, the U.S. had a monopoly on the most powerful weapon in the world and had proven it could use it. The nation felt invincible, the Soviet Union felt threatened, and much of America's unfolding military, political, and economic policy was based on this fact, even as other nations gradually developed the bomb.

A memo by the Joint Chiefs of Staff in October 1945 established the central role of nuclear weapons in the Cold War: "In the foreseeable future [the bomb] will be primarily a strategic weapon of destruction against concentrated industrial areas vital to the war effort of an enemy nation. In addition, it may be employed against centers of population with a view to forcing an enemy state to yield through terror and disintegration of national morale. . . . The bomb is not in general a tactical weapon suitable for employment against ground troops or naval forces at sea, because they offer targets too widely dispersed to justify the use of a weapon of such limited availability and great cost."

Killing civilians had become not just an unfortunate byproduct of war; because it was economical, it had become the whole point of war. You could threaten entire cities with extinction without actually pulling the trigger. (This is where the expression "getting more bang for the buck" originates.) The Joint Chiefs targeted twenty Soviet cities, each with more than six hundred thousand people. Even after nuclear weapons proliferated and became smaller and more portable, a total-war policy prevailed. The U.S. had invincibility at a relatively low cost, a monopoly on the most terrible weapon ever made, and seemingly effortless economic growth. America in the forties was now the mightiest nation on earth.

An Atomic Society

The nation was strong, but the weapon, paradoxically, made Americans feel vulnerable. The dropping of the atomic bomb had severe social, psychic, and cultural consequences that shattered the American self-image. Within days of Hiroshima, "all the major elements of our contemporary engagement with the nuclear reality took shape. . . . The entire basis of . . . existence . . . fundamentally altered," says commentator Paul Boyer. Fear, panic, hysteria, apathy,

dreams of utopia, and moral confusion swept America. Sociologists worried that the U.S. had mass suicidal tendencies. All this was despite the fact that the country was the victor and that it alone owned the bomb.

As early as August 9, 1945, a torrent of ink poured from every newspaper and magazine, expressing fears of the atomic weapon. *Reader's Digest* ran stories such as "What the Atomic Bomb Would Do to Us" and "Mist of Death Over New York." Newspapers predicted the imminent death of the entire human race. The end of the world was at hand, they cried, years before enough bombs existed to make such a prediction a reality. It is strange to realize that the U.S. came out of the war almost untouched, yet Americans saw themselves as potential victims of their own bomb rather than as a threat to the rest of the world.

Despite such horrible destruction, a Gallup Poll in 1946 found 85 percent of Americans approved the dropping of the bombs on Japan. Military strength won over morality. To be fair, the people didn't know the whole story. Accounts of radiation sickness killing thousands in Japan were suppressed by the American military, and reports of radiation damage emerging from Japan were dismissed as Japanese propaganda. Government censorship about radiation was standard operating procedure well into the next decade.

Atomic Culture

Early books on atomic power sought to explain the atom's role in the world and to predict its future. Many of these books shared common themes and fears, and gave amazingly

> "Since then I have hardly been able to smile, the future seems so utterly grim for our two little boys. Most of the time I have been in tears or near-tears, and [have had] fleeting but torturing regrets that I have brought children into the world to face such a dreadful thing as this."
>
> A young mother writing to radio columnist H. V. Kaltenborn after the Hiroshima bomb

accurate predictions. *Fear, War and the Bomb,* by P. M. S. Blackett (1948), called for political control of nuclear weapons. He said bomb shelters would quell public fears. He advocated smaller, more portable bombs and was aware of how the bomb changed

foreshadowing of the laser defenses being designed for the Strategic Defense Initiative (SDI), or "Star Wars," of the 1980s. Gessner G. Hawley, in *Atomic Energy in War and Peace* (1945), hoped nuclear power could bring about an American utopia;

An atomic explosion thought to be equivalent to about 50,000 tons of TNT rocked the normally tranquil waters of the Bikini Atoll on the morning of July 26, 1946. A month earlier, veteran statesman Bernard M. Baruch, the United States representative to the United Nations Atomic Energy Commission, had urged control of nuclear weapons with the assertion that, "We are here to make a choice between the quick and the dead."

conventional warfare. He talked as though the USSR had the bomb already and assumed that weapons of mass destruction were natural weapons of war. Blackett foresaw civilian uses for nuclear energy, including revolutionary advances in medicine and industrial power, and realized the impossibility of the United States retaining its nuclear monopoly.

Atomic Energy in the Coming Era, by David Dietz (1945), is notable for being one of the earliest discussions of potential defensive weapons against nuclear bombs, an incredibly early

he foresaw atomic energy substituting for fossil fuels and envisioned medical applications for atomic energy.

The word "atomic" quickly entered the collective vocabulary. Businesses used the word in their names; toys promised atomic powers; atomic power and sexual allure even linked up when two-piece bathing suits were named bikinis, after the place where the powerful atom bombs were first tested — on the Bikini Atoll, in the Pacific, in 1946.

Despite the hysteria in the media, Americans' fears were less out in the open. An important early survey of Americans' nuclear attitudes by Cottrell and Eberhart (1948) asked questions about the morality of the bomb. A full two-thirds believed that atomic bombs would someday be used against the U.S. The most revealing finding of the survey was that people felt a lack of control over the atomic bomb. The general response was "there is no use worrying over something you can't do anything about."

The sense of futility was fed by an information campaign to quell fears of radiation by making it seem like just one more calculated risk of war. Calls for civil defense plans also produced a false sense of security, culminating in 1950 with the mass market publication of *How to Survive an Atomic Bomb,* by Richard Gerstell. The campaign, full of false information, diminished the hysteria into resignation. Psychologists called this phenomenon "psychic numbing."

There was little examination in the press of whether it was right or wrong to drop the bomb, since most felt America was justified. Occasionally, some religious leaders voiced moral doubts. Some in the African-Amercan community, such as the poet Langston Hughes, believed that the bombing was racially motivated. The Germans had been spared, but the Japanese, those "yellow jackets" as they were portrayed in the American media, were not. These voices were seen as unpatriotic in light of Japanese harsh treatment of the Allies during the war.

Control of the Bomb

Many Americans immediately called for international control of atomic weapons. The United

Nations, formed in June 1945, became an early center of nuclear control advocacy. At the first meeting of the United Nations Atomic Energy Commission on June 13, 1946, U.S. delegate Bernard Baruch proposed a plan for international control of atomic energy. Here was the United States, the first and only country to use the bomb, being the first to say it should never be used again by anyone. Despite the Baruch plan's popularity at the United Nations, Americans ultimately favored keeping their nuclear monopoly and refused, despite pressure from the UN, to share its nuclear secrets, especially as the Cold War heated up.

Bikini Atoll

America's initial hysteria over the bomb subsided when, almost a year after Hiroshima and Nagasaki, the United States exploded the first postwar nuclear bombs in tests at the Bikini Atoll in the Marshall Islands, in the South Pacific, in July 1946. The prospect of witnessing a nuclear explosion firsthand galvanized the media. Fears of global destruction from these two detonations rang from the radio, briefly renewing national hysteria. But the weapon fell two miles off target, and observers saw little. This anticlimax did much to quell public fears about the effects of the bomb.

The second bomb at Bikini was an underwater test. This got much less attention from the media but had long-term effects on the local ecology and health of the Bikini islanders. The surrounding waters and atmosphere were contaminated with deadly radioactive fallout, described in morbid detail in the bestseller, *No Place to*

"Seldom if ever has a war ended leaving the victors with such a sense of uncertainty and fear, with such a realization that the future is obscure and that survival is not assured."

Edward R. Murrow, CBS broadcast on August 12, 1945

Klaus Fuchs had been a member of the German Communist party before fleeing the country in the 1930s. He was appointed to the Manhattan Project to develop the first atomic bomb, but from the start was passing the project's secrets to Soviet secret agents. Arrested and convicted in 1950, on his eventual release in 1959, he became director of the Institute of Nuclear Physics in East Germany.

Hide, by Dr. David Bradley, a physician who had observed the explosions. Death from radiation, not the explosion itself, became the American public's new fear.

Klaus Fuchs, Spy

On September 29, 1945, the United States secretly brought in sixteen German scientists, so-called Reich technicians, to work on the atomic bomb. By the end of 1948, a total of 457 German scientists had come to the United States. German refugee Klaus Fuchs, a British citizen, worked on the Manhattan Project in 1944, spying for the Soviets and giving them top-secret designs for the hydrogen bomb, a weapon even more powerful than the first atomic bomb. Fuchs was tried and convicted in January 1950, spending nine years in a U.S. prison (after which he moved to East Germany and became a member of the Communist party).

Four days after Fuchs's conviction, President Truman ordered the Atomic Energy Commission to complete the hydrogen bomb in order to stay ahead of the Soviets, who, it was feared, could now build the weapon using information given to them by Fuchs. However, documents recently discovered by Daniel Hirsch and William G. Mathews show that early research on the hydrogen bomb was faulty and that Fuchs had unknowingly passed this erroneous information to the Soviets. Their evidence indicates that the Soviets developed the H-bomb, not from Fuchs's information, but from monitoring radioactive fallout from the first American H-bomb test in 1951, a situation J. Robert Oppenheimer had warned about in 1947 during his testimony before the House Un-American Activities Committee (HUAC).

Nuclear Proliferation and Power

The Soviet Union tested its first atomic bomb in August 1949. Americans, by now used to the idea of nuclear annihilation, did not at first comprehend the Soviet nuclear threat. For four years, America had been the sole nuclear power, and its nuclear arsenal was relatively small.

Now, with the Soviets capable of threatening the U.S. with nuclear bombs, the country went wholeheartedly into the nuclear bomb business. The devices grew bigger and more numerous in the hopes of staying ahead of the enemy. This spurred the Soviet Union to increase its arsenal — and the superpower arms race was on. The climate of fear and suspicion in the Cold War only escalated each time the superpowers added to their nuclear arsenals. What, many Americans wondered, was the point of having all these weapons if mutually assured destruction prevented their use in the first place?

Nuclear energy was less sensational than nuclear bombs, but it was a byproduct of them. Announcing the bombing of Hiroshima, President Truman concluded: "Atomic energy may in the future supplement the power that now comes from coal, oil and falling water, but at present it cannot be produced on a basis to compete with them commercially. Before that comes there must be a long period of intensive research." But with relative speed, by 1949, nuclear power plants, called breeder reactors, became a reality in Tennessee, Illinois, and New York, with more planned for other states. Questions of toxic pollution from spent nuclear fuel had not yet arisen: Nuclear power looked like the answer to expensive fossil fuels. From the first fissionable uranium 235 isolated in 1940 to the great atom smashers producing three hundred million volts in 1945 and the arrival of nuclear power plants in 1949, the forties were the first decade in which the nuclear menace and the power of science became unavoidable facts of life for all Americans.

The Iron Curtain

America's power seemed incontestable in 1945, but its relationship with the Soviet Union was crumbling over the balance of power in postwar Europe. Truman, despite Stalin's threatening words at Potsdam, at first found it difficult to view the USSR as the enemy until February 9, 1946, when Stalin gave a speech claiming that communism and capitalism were incompatible and the world economy would have to be transformed along Communist lines.

Then came Winston Churchill's famous speech at Fulton, Missouri, in March, 1946, warning that "an iron curtain had descended" across Europe. Said Churchill, "Throughout the world, communist parties constitute a growing challenge and peril to Christian civilization. I do not believe that Soviet Russia desires war. What

Wartime British Prime Minister Winston Churchill delivering his chilling "iron curtain" speech, "The Sinews of Peace," in March, 1946. He called for the United States and Britain to unite against a potential Soviet enemy that desired "the indefinite expansion of [its] power and doctrine."

I am convinced there is nothing they [the Soviets] so much admire as strength, and there is nothing for which they have less respect than weakness, especially military weakness . . . .

But what we have to consider here today, while time remains, is the permanent prevention of war and the establishment of conditions of freedom and democracy as rapidly as possible in all countries."

Former British Prime Minister Winston Churchill in his "Iron Curtain" speech

they desire is the fruits of war and the indefinite expansion of their power and doctrines." When the USSR staged a brutal coup in Czechoslovakia by throwing its president, Jan Masaryk, out of a window, the world began to believe him.

The Eastern Bloc

For his part, Stalin feared the possibility of a renewed German threat on his western frontier. But he also feared a general expansion of other western European countries in his direction and a subsequent weakening of communism. Thus was born Stalin's idea for the Eastern Bloc. Where Communist governments did not exist, the Soviet Union helped create them, forming a tightly held sphere of influence that increased their strength and reduced their vulnerability.

Thus the early Cold War focused on eastern Europe. At first, the Soviet Army had occupied much of the region in order to liberate it from the Nazis. On Stalin's orders, the army stayed to add muscle to the formation of Communist governments in those satellite countries. The United States tried through diplomacy, using Truman's Open Door Policy (which said that eastern Europe should be allowed freedom of self-determination), to convince these eastern European countries to democratize, but diplomacy was no match for the occupying Red Army's strength.

Politically as well as symbolically, the Red Army occupation of eastern Europe, the division of Germany, and the failure of the Open Door Policy put communism on increasingly firm ground. By decade's end, the Soviet sphere included East Germany, Poland, Czechoslovakia, Hungary,

After World War II, Europe was clearly divided between the Communist East and the democratic West. The "iron curtain" had been drawn.

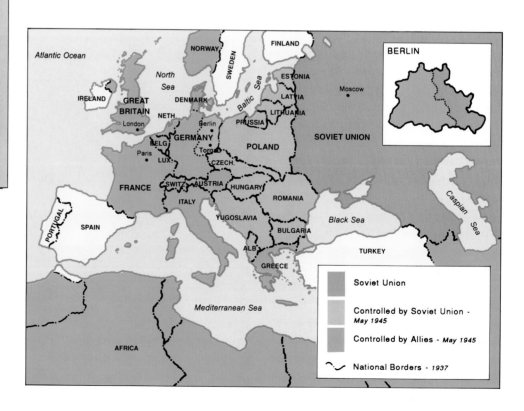

Romania, Bulgaria, Albania, and, until 1948, Yugoslavia. Truman saw Soviet expansion as outright aggression against former allies. He knew it had to be stopped.

The Policy of Containment

Despite Truman's strident tone with Stalin, an all-out ground war in eastern Europe was not an option immediately after World War II. For one thing, a sufficient nuclear arsenal did not yet exist to make Stalin back down. For another, the United States was not seeking territory for itself but instead wanted political influence, as did the Soviet Union. Also, despite rising anticommunist sentiments, Americans did not want a war with the USSR, which had been a loyal ally in the recent war.

Truman's solution was a diplomatic one that would change the way American presidents made foreign policy for the rest of the century. Truman said, "I believe that it must be the policy of the United States to support free peoples who are resisting attempted subjugation by armed minorities or by outside pressures." By "outside pressures" he meant the Soviet Union's push into eastern Europe. With this simple statement, he created the Truman Doctrine: the idea of giving aid to countries to buy their allegiance, establish democracy, and thus prevent the spread of communism into eastern Europe.

By 1947, U.S. influence in eastern Europe had slipped away. Other parts of Europe, where economic and political distress created fertile territory for Communist expansion, particularly in Greece and Turkey, became the focus of the Truman Doctrine. In a 1947 issue of *Foreign Affairs* magazine, George Kennan, U.S. ambassador to the Soviet Union, called for a firm stance against Soviet pressure in western Europe. This deceptively simple concept was the keystone of the most far-reaching foreign policy created in the second half of the twentieth century, the policy of containment. This was the idea that communism's spread could be contained and prevented through political means. Instead of armed warfare, communism would be held back by a regular policy of aiding economically weak democracies and other allies, and using the presence of nuclear weapons in allied countries to deter Soviet expansion.

How Real Was the Communist Threat?

Containment puzzled Americans. A former ally was now an archrival, and the Soviet Union seemed bent on Communist domination and democracy's downfall, although, in fact, the Soviet Union did not have the military or economic capability to take over the world. The nuclear threat only exacerbated the problem.

But the USSR, with its inefficient state-run economy, could not provide both arms for its military and food for its people. Opting for guns meant a rapid decline in the living standard for Soviet citizens and a repressive government that outlawed free markets. Given America's nuclear superiority, its recent military victory, and the Truman Doctrine, the Soviet Union believed with some justification that the U.S. aimed to destroy communism.

> ### COMMUNISM
>
> For further information see primary source entries on pages
>
> **11:** 1511-13, 1571-82;
> **12:** 1596-1602, 1605-11

The CIA

If not destroy it, then America certainly hoped to weaken the Soviet threat. To help do this, the National Security Act of 1947 established the Central Intelligence Agency (CIA), at first headed by Rear Admiral Sidney W. Souers. It was the first time the U.S. openly and legally permitted spying against any foreign powers.

The CIA's predecessor was the Office of Strategic Services (OSS), a wartime intelligence unit headed by the colorful and erratic William Donovan. Donovan coveted the role of CIA director, which he soon attained. Truman, like Roosevelt before him, was wary of the CIA, not least because he regarded Donovan as a unpredictable and self-centered gossip.

Truman feared the CIA could become a Gestapo-like arm of the government. To keep the CIA from having too much power, Truman formed the National Security Council, a group of close presidential advisors, to oversee CIA activities. The council insisted on a balance of military and civilian components in the CIA to avoid military dominance; it also limited the CIA's activities to foreign matters, which made it politically more palatable in the U.S. This kept in place other domestic intelligence services, such as the FBI and the U.S. Information Agency, creating unfortunate duplication and waste. The secrecy in the CIA grew out of Cold War tensions and also fed them. As the Soviets perfected their own espionage tactics, the CIA countered and its budgets grew accordingly.

The Marshall Plan

Just as the CIA grew in size and expense, so did the Cold War. Implementation of the Truman Doctrine began on March 4, 1947, with the

William J. "Wild Bill" Donovan (center, right), a World War I congressman and Medal of Honor winner, became the first head of the Office of Strategic Services (OSS), in June 1942. The United States was the last major power to develop an intelligence service.

The Marshall Plan of the late forties and early fifties was intended to rebuild Europe as an eastern bulwark against communism and to put the European economies back on their feet quickly. In part, the Plan was also a way Europeans could rapidly begin buying U.S. exports again. Wanting to avoid a repetition of the chaos in Europe that resulted from World War I, America poured $17 billion into war-torn Europe, in Secretary of State George C. Marshall's words, to "[break] the vicious circle and [restore] the confidence of the European people in the economic future of . . . Europe as a whole."

Marshall Plan devised by Truman's Secretary of State, George C. Marshall, to aid all former warring nations, including the Soviet Union and the Eastern Bloc (which refused to accept this aid).

The Marshall Plan aimed to bolster European economies and create healthy trading partnerships with the United States. Mutual economic benefits came first. Under the Marshall Plan, $400 million went to Greece to prevent civil war in March 1947, and in June, Europe and China also received aid. Between 1948 and 1951, $17 billion was spent to rebuild war-torn Europe. This investment eventually formed the basis of the European Community, America's major trading partner.

The money did bring about non-communist rulers in Greece and Turkey. Unfortunately, it also helped put in power in those two countries right-wing governments that were insensitive to the civil and human rights of their own people. But as long as these governments were not allied to the Soviets, the U.S. did not really worry a great deal about it. All America asked in return from these governments was proof that its beneficiaries used the money they were granted to rebuild their economies.

Cold War Diplomacy

The Truman Doctrine, the Marshall Plan, and the policy of containment made Truman the master foreign diplomat and strategist. Whenever and wherever communism confronted American interests, Truman met it head on. His diplomatic feats punctuated the decade.

Children cheer as another American military plane arrives carrying supplies to blockaded West Berlin. The city was divided between the Soviets and the western Allies at the end of the war. In 1947, Stalin, fearing a consolidation of the western part of the city against the eastern half, blockaded the German capital. Its two and one half million people were kept alive largely by the twenty-five hundred tons of food airlifted daily by America and its allies.

In 1947, Truman participated in signing the Rio Pact, leading to the formation of the Organization of American States in 1948. This alliance of the United States with the larger nations in the Americas created a bond in the western hemisphere.

Truman also handled the Berlin Airlift crisis of 1947-48. The western allies occupying Berlin's western zones had unified into one zone. Stalin, fearing the solidification of western power at his back door, blockaded Berlin. Calling Stalin's bluff, Truman ordered an airlift of supplies to the besieged city. The action raised Europe's morale by seeing the Soviet Union foiled and also saved many lives in the starving city.

The Brussels Pact of western European nations in 1948 provided another opportunity in the fight against possible Communist expansion. Responding to a Communist uprising in Czechoslovakia and Communist parties springing up in Italy and France, Truman introduced the Vandenburg Resolution, which articulated the democratic principles of and the program for mutual aid set out in the Marshall Plan.

The creation of the North Atlantic Treaty Organization (NATO) in 1949 was one of the more significant alliances in which Truman played a part. NATO was the first military alliance the United States had ever joined in peacetime and was also the first time in a century and a half that the U.S. made a political alliance with any European power.

On October 1, 1949, Mao Zedong proclaimed the establishment of the Communist People's Republic of China. Right-wingers in Congress immediately put the blame on the Democratic administration for failing to support America's nationalist ally in China, Chiang Kai-shek. The truth, however, was that Chiang's corrupt government had lost the support of the Chinese people, especially in the rural areas, who had been easily attracted to the Communist cause. This Chinese poster shows the Communist troops' triumphant entry into Peking in January 1949.

NATO included the United States, Canada, and twelve western European countries. It was a military coopera-tive, responsible for nuclear and con-ventional military strategy in Europe to resist Communist expansion. Thus, the door was opened to U.S. military assistance to Europe and the Americas on a vast scale.

Yet containment failed in China in 1949, when Chiang Kai-Shek's government fell to Mao Zedong's Communist revolution. U.S. paranoia over Communist infiltration grew; many blamed Truman for Chiang's fall despite ten years of American aid. The fall of China meant the loss of an important ally.

Truman cheerfully displays the erroneous headline in the Chicago Daily Tribune of November 4, 1948, while on his victorious return trip to Washington D.C. His whistlestop campaign tour, where he decried the Republicans as "bloodsuckers with offices on Wall Street, princes of privilege, plunderers," probably swung the outcome for Truman.

"Once they get movies throttled, how long before we're told what we can say . . . into a radio microphone?"

Frank Sinatra, singer, 1947

Truman Defeats Dewey

On the domestic front, Harry Truman also faced serious challenges. By a slim margin, Truman won the 1948 election in a surprise victory over Republican Thomas E. Dewey, governor of New York. So certain had Dewey's victory seemed that, even before all the votes were counted, newspapers printed headlines screaming "Dewey Defeats Truman!" An also-ran in the presidential race was Henry Wallace, who had once been considered for FDR's running mate in 1944. Wallace ran as an independent candidate who preached that socialism should not be feared; he was naturally painted as a Communist sympathizer.

To win in this increasingly conservative era, Truman had to walk a moderate line. He was a victim of his own success as an anticommunist abroad. There were also rising antiliberal senti-ments at home, where he was deserted by the extreme left- and right-wing members of his own party. Support from FDR's old New Deal coalition was not enough to push through his own liberal reform program, the Fair Deal, which many portrayed as communism. Throughout the late forties, Republicans and conservative Democrats in Congress crushed Truman's efforts to pass laws on civil rights, housing, education, and labor. For instance, the Taft-Hartley Act strengthening employers' rights in labor disputes was vetoed by Truman, but overridden by Congress. One of Truman's few domestic legislative successes was a housing reform law passed in 1949.

The Red Menace

The expansion of communism in Europe and China and Truman's policy of containment fed a rising hysteria

J. Edgar Hoover. (1895-1972)

A lawyer by training, John Edgar Hoover had one of the century's longest careers in government — forty-eight years — spanning every president from Coolidge to Nixon. Entering the Justice Department in 1917 and becoming director of the Federal Bureau of Investigation in 1924, Hoover remained director of the nation's top security agency until his death. By that time, he had been honored by literally dozens of organizations or universities, and was one of the most powerful men in Washington, a much-feared fixture on the political landscape who surrounded himself in mystery.

As director of the FBI, Hoover ran a tight ship, and was exceedingly (and later, excessively) diligent in his investigations. Hoover also went out of his way to support state and local police training and is generally credited with raising the national standards of police work. In the twenties, he expanded the technical role of the FBI by instituting fingerprint files and, in the thirties, he established the FBI's crime laboratory. The lab became a national resource in tracking America's gangsters and mobsters of the day. His fight against this riffraff made him a national hero.

During wartime, Hoover and his agency were some of President Roosevelt's main domestic security watchdogs, a position the FBI relished. Before FDR even imagined incarcerating 110,000 Japanese-American citizens in March 1942, Hoover had drafted a list of Japanese aliens he believed required detention. Thus began Hoover's intensive wartime effort to guard against enemy spies in America.

"We're about as much in favor of Communism as J. Edgar Hoover."

Humphrey Bogart and Lauren Bacall

During the late forties and fifties, Hoover played a central role in Cold War politics, shifting the FBI's investigations from violent crime to Communist subversion. Hoover had long cloaked his agency in an impermeable secrecy that verged on paranoia. However, with the real or imagined Communist threat, Hoover became downright obsessive. Under his command, many Americans were placed under FBI surveillance — including First Lady Eleanor Roosevelt, whom Hoover distrusted for her advocacy of black civil rights and her friendship with leftist liberals. On some of these individuals, Hoover even kept secret dossiers full of illegally obtained information and personal details.

Hoover brought to his position a deep-seated hatred of Communists and African-Americans. A racist, he abused his power, finding ways to suppress the black civil rights protests of Marcus Garvey, Martin Luther King, Jr., and everyone in between. Hoover's defense of American security was thus full of paradoxes and contradictions; he was a fiercely patriotic champion of democracy while persecuting anyone whose beliefs were not in line with his own.

Hoover's public image was more benevolent, though it tied in with his deeply held suspicion of outsiders. He took it upon himself to be a spokesperson for traditional values, instructing the nation in morals, family ties, religion, and the importance of obeying those in authority. In Hoover's mind, national security and sound morals in the American home were inseparable.

Not until after Hoover's death was the FBI's rampant abuse of power made public, and his public image become tarnished. For fifty years, he had appeared as a heroic figure in the fight to preserve democracy against outside forces, but his heroism was a smoke screen, in large part created by the man himself.

that Communists were infiltrating the United States government. Communist subversion was suspected at every level of American leadership. Despite Truman's Fair Deal, he swung with the conservative mood, ordering

The 1949-50 trial of State Department official Alger Hiss symbolizes the fears aroused at the time by the Cold War. Though he consistently denied the accusations that he had passed secret documents to Whittaker Chambers, a self-confessed Communist party courier, he was nevertheless convicted of perjury and sentenced to five years' imprisonment.

loyalty checks of all federal employees. Thousands of loyalty checks were carried out on the flimsiest reports of Communist sympathies, and suspicion replaced evidence. The effort yielded only a small percentage of actual dismissals. No evidence was found of large-scale Communist subversion of the government. All the loyalty checks did was add to the atmosphere of rising fear.

In this charged atmosphere, the House Un-American Activities Committee escalated its activities in 1947, investigating the atomic scientists and even many famous Hollywood figures for the slightest hint of Communist activity. The aura of a witch hunt permeated the proceed-

ings, resulting in the circulation of long blacklists of Hollywood writers, directors, and actors forbidden to work ever again in their professions because of their alleged political beliefs. The Hollywood Ten, a group of blacklisted writers, citing their First Amendment rights, were even jailed for refusing to testify before Congress about alleged Communist activity in the film industry. By the end of the decade, even America's colleges and universities were considered likely spawning grounds of Communist sympathizers.

Alger Hiss

Nobody was immune to charges of Communist conspiracy. In 1949, Alger Hiss, a former New Dealer in the State Department and a close compatriot of FDR, was accused by Whittaker Chambers (once a member of a Communist spy ring himself) of passing classified documents to the Soviets. Hiss made an unlikely Communist. He was from a wealthy old northeastern family and had been the secretary general of the United Nations Organizing Conference from 1945 to 1946. Conservatives blamed Hiss for aiding FDR in bargaining away eastern Europe at the Yalta conference. In such a political climate, the case came to trial before the HUAC, a member of which was Representative Richard M. Nixon. Hiss denied all the charges and was later acquitted.

To clear the damage done to his reputation, Alger Hiss in turn brought a libel suit against Whittaker Chambers. At this trial, Chambers brought out private details of Hiss's life that seemed to implicate Hiss as having been a Communist spy after all. But as the statute of limitations on espionage had expired (the alleged events surrounding both men having happened in the thirties), Hiss lost his suit. At a third trial, Hiss was tried again, this time for perjury for lying to Congress about his alleged spying activities, and was convicted in January of 1950. He was sentenced to five years in prison. In this much-debated case, it is still not known for certain whether Hiss was actually a Soviet spy.

Communists in America

There were, of course, Communists in America, but not very many. They were hunted down by the FBI,

blacklisted, jailed, and generally persecuted for their political beliefs. The media portrayed them as degenerate, immoral, and psychologically unbalanced, especially the Communist women. Communist women in America were portrayed as unclean, old maidish, and ugly, or else as tempting seductresses and sexual deviants who used their feminine wiles to recruit hapless American men into the party.

Yet despite the hysteria over the red menace in the late forties, the average American did not seriously regard communism as a great threat. Between 1947 and 1953, the results of a national poll showed that no more than 18 percent of those asked put Communism at the top of the nation's list of domestic problems.

A decorated truck leads a marching unit down Eighth Avenue past Pennsylvania Station, in New York City, as part of the Communist sponsored May Day Parade on April 30, 1949. Carrying placards reading "End the Cold War," the paraders also voiced opposition to the Marshall Plan and the bomb. The truck carrying children shows the slogan, "We don't want another war. We want our daddies to stay at home."

CHAPTER 5
Life in Postwar America

Homecoming

When war ended, the troops came flooding home. Seventy thousand soldiers and sailors per month were demobilized and reintroduced to American society. For many veterans, the war had left physical, emotional, and psychological scars, as portrayed in the 1946 movie *The Best Years of Our Lives*. Yet, however high the cost, whether America's soldiers returned injured or not, they were returning home as victorious heroes.

As early as 1943, economists started planning how veterans would reenter the work force. In an economic manual of 1944, J. Douglas Brown said, "The men returning from the armed services, will . . . constitute the finest body of manpower the world has ever seen." True enough, but how to employ it in a peacetime economy? And what would happen to the millions of women and African-Americans their reemployment threatened to displace? And where, with a severe housing shortage, would they all live? The joy of victory rapidly gave way to apprehension as these economic uncertainties loomed.

The GI Bill of Rights

The government's answer to these questions was the Servicemen's Readjustment Act, or the GI Bill of Rights. The bill provided low-cost home mortgages to veterans, setting off a

During World War II, housing starts slowed to a trickle, and the returning GIs wanted security, jobs, and new homes for their families. In 1947, the first and most famous planned community in the United States was created out of farmland on Long Island, New York. In Levittown, all the houses had a living room with a fireplace, two bedrooms, and a large attic that could be converted to make two extra bedrooms.

As the suburbs grew and new industries developed, the consumer society flourished. This Frigidaire ad for General Motors ensures every housewife would covet refrigeration in the kitchen.

boom in construction and its related industries. Between 1948 and 1958, a total of thirteen million new homes were built. (Obviously, not all of them were built with GI Bill money alone.)

The suburbs flourished as people escaped overcrowded cities for the paradise of their own home and a plot of land. Entire prefabricated suburban towns such as Levittown, Long Island, the brainchild of developer William J. Levitt, sprang up. Each house in this tract housing project (a housing development on a large tract of land, built by a real estate developer) had its own amenities, yet was comforting in its similarity to its neighbors. It was a housing recipe that was much copied from then on.

The construction boom set off a domino effect in the home appliance and furnishing industries. Shopping centers sprang up to cater to the new suburbs, creating a boom in the auto industry as people had to drive greater distances to shop. This, in turn, spurred the industries related to the auto, including fuel, rubber, parts, tools, and plastics. The suburbs had become the new frontier.

Two former soldiers who benefited from the 1944 GI Bill of Rights emerge from Wheeler Hall at the University of California, Berkeley. By 1947, more than four million war veterans had taken advantage of the opportunities in housing, business, and education provided by the bill.

The GI Bill also paid for several years of college and provided low-cost business loans. For the young men who had put their families, careers, and lives on hold to serve their country, the GI Bill was their key to reestablishing themselves. Millions of young men went to college on the GI Bill. Higher education, a rarity before the war, was now available to many, not just to the rich and privileged few. The GI Bill increased the percentage of Americans attending college over two generations and led to the expansion of America's entire education system. In 1940, for example, 109,000 men and 77,000 women graduated from college with B.A. degrees. By 1949, that number almost tripled to 328,000 men, and 103,000 women.

Economic Transition

The GI Bill was ingenious, but it could not solve the larger economic problems caused by the war. Postwar prosperity was in part offset by consumer shortages and high inflation. Within a year of the war's end, the rate of inflation had tripled, then it doubled the following year.

Another major problem was the conversion of the American war industry, which had for four years been the driving force in the economy. Now the U.S. had to convert almost 70 percent of its production from wartime to peacetime products (compared with 30 percent after World War I). The $100 billion economy now had to be transformed somehow from a wartime to a peacetime footing, yet still retain the military-industrial complex that was emerging out of the Cold War.

Factories scrambled to retool, worried about being caught with large and unnecessary weapons inventories. Businesses hurriedly tried to plan or guess what postwar markets wanted, and feared losing their profits. Another question was whether the government would continue to control the economy to the degree it had in wartime, and if so, what form this control would take. The government had indeed become bloated since 1940. The federal budget had gone from $13.2 billion in 1940 to $39.6 billion in 1949. In that time, the national debt rose from $43 billion to $257.4 billion. Fair Dealers such as Truman indicated that this inflationary trend was set to continue well beyond the end of the war.

Labor Unrest

Postwar economic chaos was fed by growing labor unrest. Union membership had doubled during the forties, and unemployment was under 4 percent. But uneasiness about the economy produced tension between

In 1946, 4.6 million American workers went on strike, losing business 113 million working days. Largest among the striking numbers were the 750,000 U.S. Steel workers, whose three-week strike gained them an 18.5 percent wage hike. Meanwhile, the demands of the striking coal miners included health, welfare, and safety benefits. Despite fears that the strikes would lead to violence, serious strife was avoided.

The Taft-Hartley Act of 1947 rolled back some of the gains made by workers under the New Deal. The act was strongly fought by the big unions, the American Federation of Labor describing it as "conceived in a spirit of vindictiveness." Truman vetoed the bill, but the veto was overidden in the Senate by a vote of sixty-eight to twenty-five and the act was passed. Here, Senate Secretary Carl A. Loeffler (center) signs the bill as Representative Fred A. Hartley (left), and Senator Robert A. Taft look on.

labor and management, sparking an era of gigantic strikes for job security and wage increases. For example, in 1946, 750,000 steelworkers went on strike as did 200,000 workers at General Electric. The national telephone strike of 1946 involved 240,000 union women demanding equal pay. In 1948, 350,000 coal miners went on strike, and in 1949, 500,000 steelworkers followed.

These strikes made wages rise. For the first time, labor contracts included cost-of-living increases. This rise in wages fueled buying power and consumer demand, and thus pushed greater production and business expansion. With greater economic power, the unions also became more politically powerful, more friendly toward management, and more involved in Democratic party politics.

But with the unions' new power, management feared rising production costs and the diminution of its own power. The Taft-Hartley Act of 1947,

passed over Truman's veto, was business's answer to the unions as it allowed states to enact labor laws that differed from federal labor law. The states' labor laws gave management more power over workers and discouraged union organizing, which management viewed as dangerously radical. Under Taft-Hartley, union leaders had to pledge that they were not Communists. The act almost totally stifled the unions' power, rendering them virtually impotent.

The general population's average salary also rose, nearly tripling between 1940 and 1949. Lessons learned from the Depression and the planned economy of World War II led to the introduction of the Full Employment Bill of 1945 and its passage as the Employment Act of 1946. This law made stable prices and full employment a policy goal of the U.S. government, though in reality, these objectives were never fully met in the postwar boom years.

Postwar Roles of Women and African-Americans

Labor unrest was further stirred up by the reentry of millions of white male veterans into the workforce, throwing millions of women and black workers out of high paying jobs and into minimum-wage service positions, or, as in most cases, out of work altogether. In this era before antidiscrimination laws, management deliberately laid off women first, then African-Americans, strictly on the basis of sex and race, not skill or seniority. Women in highly trained and specialized factory jobs, such as welding and shipbuilding, were flatly turned down for new positions in their field because they were women. This meant a sudden and drastic loss

of income. It led to frustrating job searches with stiff competition, taking a lesser paying job, or selecting a new field entirely from a limited range of choices.

According to Helen Baker in *The Readjustment of Manpower*, written before the end of the war, the lay-off of women and blacks was planned, much as their wartime integration had been: "Executives . . . are counting on the widespread withdrawal of women from the labor market. . . . Voluntary withdrawal is hoped for. . . . In other cases, separate seniority lists, rules against the employment of married women, the limitation of women's employment to prewar jobs and other specific discriminatory devices will be resorted to." This discrimination, Baker explained, was based not on a difference in efficiency between the sexes but rather on the feeling on the part of both management and union

"[A woman must] accept herself fully as a woman [and] know . . . she is dependent on a man. There is no fantasy in her mind about being an independent woman, a contradiction in terms."

Marynia Farnham and Ferdinand Lundberg in *Modern Woman*

Discrimination and segregation continued despite the gains made by African-Americans during the war years. In this 1948 photograph, a black student, G. W. McLaurin, is forced to sit apart from his fellow undergraduates at the University of Oklahoma. A Supreme Court ruling had forced the institution to accept McLaurin as a student, but the school insisted that segregation had to be maintained.

Adam Clayton Powell. (1908-1984)

Adam Clayton Powell was the flamboyant minister who, in 1945, became New York's first African-American congressman. He was only the fourth black elected to the House of Representatives in the twentieth century, largely due to congressional districts being drawn to lessen the effect of the black vote. Coming from an upper middle-class background and a graduate of Columbia University, Powell succeeded his father as minister of the Abyssinian Baptist Church in Harlem. From this loyal constituency of ten thousand, Powell established the core of his political power. Meanwhile, he amassed wealth by buying Harlem real estate.

Powell's interest in politics was inspired by Marcus Garvey, from whom he learned the leadership skills needed for a mass movement. Powell had a lot to overcome to knit together an African-American community split by economic class and weakened by hopelessness. But Powell had organizational genius and huge political ambitions. He spoke of whites and white institutions as the enemy and was thus one of the earliest activists to use race-based rhetoric to bind various black groups together.

A large part of Powell's persuasiveness was in his speech. Practiced in preaching the word of God, he also used his verbal gifts to rally African-Americans to his cause. Openly attacking whites, he identified himself with blacks who were agitating for better jobs and housing and was one of the first to use boycotts and picket lines to achieve his goals. Powell created the *People's Voice* in 1942, a mouthpiece for his politics, and often led picket lines and rallies for civil rights causes.

In 1941, Powell used his broad-based Harlem support to become the first African-American ever elected to the New York City Council, and then to the United States House of Representatives in 1945. As one of only two blacks in Congress, Powell did not endear himself to his white colleagues, whose entrenched authority he made a habit of confronting. He particularly attacked racist members of Congress, refusing to make himself one of the club. Powell stirred up a lot of bitter name calling and character bashing between himself and his white colleagues and made little headway in securing material gains for his constituency, as his refusal to compromise brought few results in his legislative efforts. Indeed, Powell flouted congressional convention even further with his poor attendance and general rebelliousness. Powell called himself "the first bad nigger in Congress," and was vain, egotistical, and exploitative of lower-class blacks' faith in him.

Powell's defects of character did not lessen his power as a symbol of the early civil rights movement, but they did backfire on his political career. Powell was ultimately excluded from Congress by his colleagues in 1967 for allegedly making improper expenditures of government funds. In a special election designed to fill his slot, he won by a landslide in 1968, but though he reattained his seat, he was deprived of his twenty-two years of seniority and was fined $25,000 for his supposed crimes. The Supreme Court, however, ruled in June, 1969, that Powell had been unconstitutionally excluded. Powell's political career officially ended in 1970, when his bid for renomination failed.

representatives that in a scarcity situation, jobs should go to the men first. "Industry . . . [will] retain men with dependents even if it is necessary to lay off women with greater seniority or with dependents."

The same story held true for African-Americans. Baker says, "As in lifting of union bans against blacks, and the total of one million African-Americans employed in war production as advancements likely to be lost after the war. The situation for black women was particularly acute, as most black women had always been the primary support for their families.

With the war over and thousands of GIs returning home to flood the labor market, women were encouraged to revert to their traditional roles of housewives and mothers. Employment and financial independence, described as feminine during the war, were now considered unwomanly.

the case of women . . . the possibility of discrimination is evidently due, not to their records as workers, but to social attitudes." E. Jay Howenstine, Jr., author of *The Economics of Demobilization* (1944), agreed: "Minority groups . . . are skeptical about the maintenance of opportunities that have become available only under the stress of war. This is particularly true of Negroes. While still severely handicapped, they have in many ways fared far better during the war than ever before." He noted higher wages, new antidiscrimination policies, the

The physically handicapped faced the same outcome at the end of the war. "In normal times," Howenstine said, "the cripple is largely junk in the eyes of industry, but the war has supplied the physically handicapped with hitherto unheard-of opportunities . . . over 200,000 . . . individuals had been trained and put to productive use in war industry." This was to be no more now that the war was over.

Of women, Howenstine asked, "Will a concerted drive be made to put the woman back in 'her place' or will the working woman . . . be given

As women were urged to return to their more "feminine" position in society, so fashion changed with the coming of the New Look. In vogue were bright colors, flouncing skirts, and polka dots. This skirt is box pleated with a "fol de rol" hip silhouette. Also fashionable once more were elaborate hats and spiky high heels. Practicality and frugality had gone out of the window.

a role becoming of her capacities in the postwar world?" These were largely rhetorical questions. For most women who held their first job during the war, its end meant a return to full-time homemaking and motherhood.

During the war, the message to women had been that their womanhood could best be expressed by going out to work and helping to win the war. Now women were hearing that work was unwomanly. Limited job opportunities and negative attitudes about women working sent them back to the home in droves. Popular books, such as *Modern Woman: The Lost Sex* by Dr. Marynia Farnham and Ferdinand Lundberg, reinforced the attitude that careers and happiness were mutually exclusive: "Abandon-

ing their feminine role has made women unhappy because it has made them frustrated. It has made children unhappy because they do not have maternal love. And it has made their husbands unhappy because they do not have real women as partners." These mixed messages sent women one powerful, overriding suggestion in itself: Your value as a person comes from how well you serve others.

Women heeded this advice, leaving the workforce entirely or taking lower-paying jobs. Women were flocking now back to the home, despite national polls showing that the vast majority of women would have preferred to continue working in their field. One group of women fought the general trend. Union women met in large numbers to discuss ways of protecting their seniority. They fought for equal pay and attempted to bring about changes in the workplace that accommodated women's dual roles as worker and mother.

Some efforts were successful. In 1945, Massachusetts became the first state with an equal pay law. The forties and fifties saw the minimum wage laws extended to include domestic and small business workers, most of whom were women. The women's bureaus of certain unions, led by their working-class membership, were some of the very few organized places in which the goals of women's equality managed to remain alive during the Cold War era.

The New Look

In keeping with women's return to traditionally feminine concerns, fashion did an about-face in 1947 with the introduction of the New

Look by Christian Dior. The style was new in name only. Gone were the practical, simple cuts and workaday suits of the war years. The New Look flaunted long, voluminous skirts, pinched-in waists, and large

dination. This was encouraged by a growing number of women's magazines, whose advertising and articles sold products by stressing the importance of a woman's appearance. By making her looks one of her primary

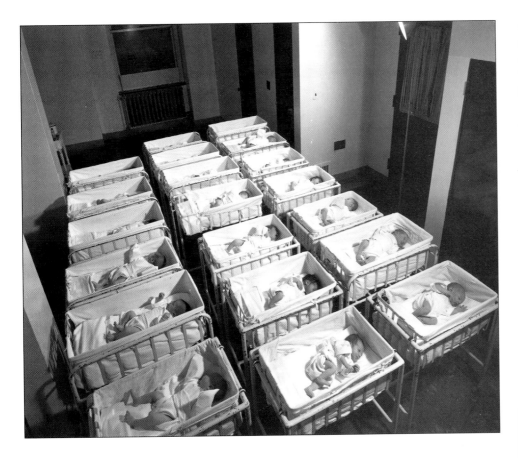

Once their wives and homes were safely secured, the next thing the returning GIs wanted was children. This gave rise to the so-called baby boom. The nation's population rose by nineteen million in the forties and by thirty million during the fifties. By 1957, one baby was born in the United States every seven seconds. Shown here is a group of newborn babies in cribs at the Beth Israel Hospital in New York City.

jutting bosoms, a virtual reinvention of Victorian femininity, exemplified by women's having to wear uncomfortable corsets and bras to achieve what evolution had not. Big, floppy hats, elaborate hairdos, spiky high heels, meticulously matched shoes, bags, and makeup: This, the fashion press screamed, was real femininity.

The New Look was not designed to aid the working woman with a busy schedule. Achieving the New Look took time. It required commitment to shopping, alterations, and outfit coor-

concerns and by manipulating her to want to fit the tight new mold, postwar American women were being restricted, both literally and symbolically, through their clothes.

The Baby Boom

Peace. The promise of plenty. Suburban expansion. Women back in the home. These factors led to one overwhelming demographic event after the war: Everyone had babies. In

"I design clothes for flower-like women, with rounded shoulders, full, feminine busts, and hand-span waists above enormous, spreading skirts."

Designer Christian Dior on his New Look of 1947

all socio-economic groups and races, marriage statistics and birthrates rose sharply. More women were having babies than ever before. Hospital wards were so overcrowded that women often went through labor in hallways. In 1926, 79 per 1,000 women gave birth; by 1946, that number leaped to 118 per 1,000. This was the baby boom. By its end in 1964, 76.4 million children had been born. This bulge in the population would affect housing, education, labor, and social trends well into the twenty-first century.

Truman's Civil Rights Committee

With the end of war and the erosion of their brief economic gains, African-Americans began to protest and agitate. The enormous black migration from rural southern to northern and western industrial states that had begun earlier in the century numbered about 160,000 people each year in the forties, bringing up social issues that previously had been isolated in the South.

As the number of blacks in formerly white areas grew, whites were confronted with racial questions unaddressed until now, in addition to the merely practical problems of trying to incorporate this large influx of people. Racial tensions began to grow, as did racism and racial segregation in response.

President Truman's Committee on Civil Rights, formed in December 1946, was a unique political answer to these racial tensions. A civil libertarian at heart, Truman appointed a diverse group of individuals, including white male corporate

leaders, labor leaders, Jews, Catholics, Protestants, college presidents, southerners, black leaders, and women, to develop the nation's first public policy to improve the status of African-Americans. "It's a big job," said Truman with characteristic bluntness to the committee, "Go to it!"

In 1947, Truman gave a speech to the NAACP (the first president ever to do so) that became a philosophical guide for the civil rights committee and gave impetus to the entire civil rights debate in the U.S. for years to come. Said Truman, "We can no longer afford the luxury of a leisurely attack upon prejudice and discrimination . . . we cannot wait another decade or another generation to remedy these evils. We must work as never before to cure them now."

The committee's effort culminated in 1947 in the report entitled "To Secure These Rights." This document espoused racial policies that equalled and even exceeded those set by the NAACP itself. The report was the basis for Truman's later executive orders desegregating the armed forces and establishing antidiscrimination policies in the federal government.

An Era of Power and Abundance

The postwar era was, in short, a time of economic and social chaos as everyone sought to resettle their lives in the face of future uncertainty. But upheaval soon turned to worldwide economic dominance, as American steel, chemical engineering, electronics, and aviation industries outstripped those in the war-ravaged

> *"[The Truman civil rights plan] wants to reduce us to the status of a mongrel, inferior race, mixed in blood, our Anglo-Saxon heritage a mockery."*
>
> Alabama governor
> F. Dixon, 1948

"'Twas the night before Christmas — the children were dreaming of a Ford in their future — smart, swanky and gleaming."

Ford advertisement, 1947

USSR, France, Britain, Japan, and Germany. Lessons learned from wartime productivity resulted in the U.S. producing half of the world's manufactured goods by 1947, almost half of its electricity, and an amazing 62 percent of its oil. Americans also owned 75 percent of the world's cars. "The promise of American capitalism was that it could produce abundance on such a scale that social problems would drown under the flood of resources," notes historian Godfrey Hodgson.

Yet, even as the United States became the wealthiest nation on earth, with a rising standard of living and unequalled power abroad, the country's social problems remained largely unresolved, reflecting a growing division between those who had and those who had not.

CHAPTER 6
Science Enters a New Age

Ambivalence Toward Progress

"The new age [that began on August 6, 1945 would change] every aspect of man's activities, from machines to morals, from physics to philosophy, from politics to poetry."

Norman Cousins, "Modern Man is Obsolete." *Saturday Review,* August 18, 1945

The atom bomb revolutionized America's attitudes toward science. Not since the industrial revolution of the mid-nineteenth century had such a fundamental technological change swept society. In the eighteenth- and nineteenth-century scientific framework, humans themselves stood apart from and were superior to the laws of nature; mid-twentieth-century views went one step further. People saw themselves as having an all-powerful influence over nature. The atomic weapon was the potent new symbol of the ultimate power of science and humanity. And yet this power dwarfed its creators.

Science was the new authority, and scientists were the high priests of the new gospel. Tying science to faith in his September 1945 message to Congress, President Truman claimed, "The events of the past few years are both proof and prophecy of what science can do."

Prior to the Manhattan Project, scientific research and invention were largely private ventures, with goals set by business rather than government. The Works Progress Administration had funded some scientific research during the Depression, setting a precedent for scientific funding during and after the war. In his address to Congress, Truman took the WPA's democratic aims a step further, raising scientific research to a government mission, saying, "The development of atomic energy is a clear-cut indication of what can be accomplished by our universities, industry, and government working together."

Ironically, this attitude toward science was helped along by the Cold War. The U.S. rethought its science policy in light of its expanded role on the world stage, and the government began to grant vast sums of money directly to universities for scientific research. This research would, it was hoped, fulfill various security and social policies. Thus, the government took a greater role in regulating and marketing scientific developments that related to public health and the environment. In medical science, the government funded research on a scale never seen before, distributing revolutionary new drugs and, during the war, recruiting virtually 100 percent of all medical school graduates into the armed services. Thus, the role of the government in science in the forties ballooned far beyond the uniform weights and measures clause spelled out in the Constitution. Science and public policy merged, never again to separate. Indeed, government's support of science only grew with the space program in the fifties and sixties.

In addition to the power of the atom itself, then, was a new kind of corporate power formed by the alliance of government and science. This put a great distance between average Americans and technology and gave rise to a popular culture that

Admiral Richard Byrd. (1888-1957)

A graduate of the U.S. Naval Academy in 1912, Richard Evelyn Byrd had been a career naval officer until a leg injury forced him to retire in 1916. Recalled to duty during World War I, he served as commander of the U.S. air forces in Canada. After the war, he directed navigational preparations for the navy's first transatlantic flight in 1919.

His first polar adventure was as commander of the navy polar expedition to Greenland in 1925. The following year, he took his first flight over the North Pole. In 1928, Byrd led the first of his five expeditions to Antarctica, which had been only spottily explored up to that time, and became the first person to fly over the South Pole itself (with this flight, he became the first person ever to have flown over both poles). For his pioneering explorations, he was promoted to rear admiral by a special act of Congress.

From 1933 through 1935, Admiral Byrd led his second voyage to Antarctica. Working under the harshest weather conditions, with little daylight and all sorts of technical difficulties due to the cold, his team discovered, mapped, and photographed vast new areas of the land and undertook scientific observations of the weather. For five months in 1934, Byrd secluded himself at a weather station 123 miles from his base camp, living underground in total solitude, during which time he almost died of carbon monoxide poisoning. He wrote about his experience in *Alone* (1938).

In 1939, President Roosevelt named Byrd to lead the U.S. Antarctic Service Exploration. It was the first time he made the trip for the government. He set up two bases and stepped up scientific projects. Byrd's work there through 1941 established American territorial interests in the region. The war years naturally interrupted this endeavor, and Byrd spent the war carrying out special assignments for the navy.

Byrd's most significant explorations of Antarctica came in 1947, when he was named officer in charge of the largest Antarctic expedition in history, an Antarctic Developments Project code-named Operation Highjump. The expedition involved thirteen ships, ski-equipped aircraft, tractors, and 4,700 men. In light of the growing Cold War, the U.S. hoped that the expedition, using icebreakers, long-range planes, and amphibious vehicles developed for the war, could use this equipment to train for polar warfare and perhaps establish a polar air base.

Richard E. Byrd and Floyd Bennett after a successful Arctic mission.

Heavy pack ice six hundred miles wide and drifting icebergs impeded the expedition's ships. Finally the ships reached their goal and began their mission: to fly over and photograph as much of the land as possible. Hundreds of mountains were spotted for the first time, along with eighteen new mountain ranges, some of them up to twenty thousand feet high. With the help of flight, radar, and photography, a total of about seventy thousand aerial mapping photographs were taken and an estimated 350,000 square miles of new lands were discovered (the size of Germany and France combined). The extensive explorations of Antarctica during this trip resulted in the mapping of the true Antarctic coast and proved Byrd's theory that it was one large continental body and not two land masses beneath the ice as had previously been thought. Byrd died in the middle of a subsequent expedition and was buried with full military honors at Arlington National Cemetery.

tried to bridge the emotional gap between them. The government repeatedly tried to alleviate Americans' fear of the bomb and the ambivalence it caused about the value of scientific progress. Indeed, Vannevar Bush, director of the Office of Scientific Research, proclaimed in 1945 that science was a path to national greatness. The media, too, consistently tried to make the terrifying power of science seem useful on the most familiar levels, promising a utopian society once the power of the atom was harnessed for everyday use.

Yet many scientific journals and newspaper editorials of the day voiced suspicions of a science that touted its great achievements when, in fact, that science had proven that it could destroy the entire world. The September 1945 issue of *Scientific Monthly* put it succinctly: "Grave doubts are in many minds, and science is being regarded with both greater respect and with greater apprehension than ever before." Tension between private morality and public science grew as citizens felt increasingly helpless to control matters of such complexity. A clear division between the common citizen and the scientific elite resulted, and many Americans turned away from science, becoming fervently anti-intellectual.

Military Contributions

Nevertheless, a great many scientific and technological advances during the forties were far-reaching. Quite a few came about because of the war and the swift growth of war-related scientific research funded by the government.

Notable developments in military technology that were later found to have civilian uses included the single-rotor helicopter. First developed in the U.S. by Igor Sikorsky in 1939, it was used with great success throughout the war because it could take off and land in unprepared sites and its vertical lift allowed it to work in confined areas without long landing strips. Improvements to the single-rotor were made by Lawrence Bell of Bell Aircraft, who received the world's first commercial helicopter license in 1946.

Jet-engine flight also advanced significantly during the war. Bell Aircraft tested the first U.S. jet plane in 1942. Propeller-driven bombers such as the B-17 Flying Fortress and B-29 Super Fortress gave way to jet-propelled aircraft after war's end. The world's largest bomber jet, the B-36, with a range of ten thousand miles, was widely produced in 1948. That same year, Captain Charles "Chuck" Yeager used jet flight to break the sound barrier.

Another military technology that came into wide use in the forties was radar, which stood for "Radio Detecting and Ranging." Radar transmitted electromagnetic impulses and detected the impulses reflected by large objects in its path, such as ships, planes, missiles, and vehicles. During the war, it was an excellent early-warning system, despite its vulnerability to jamming. After the war, radar was used in commercial aviation and shipping. Inklings of the space age took place in 1946, when the very first radar contact with the moon was made.

Other additions to ground warfare included the all-terrain jeep and, in 1942, hand-held rocket launchers, called bazookas, for use against

The helicopter, developed in the U.S. in 1939, by Igor Sikorsky, was to transform warfare and private domestic travel. This picture shows the first coast to coast flight of a commercial helicopter. The Hillier 360 lands at the Wall Street Skyport in New York City on April 12, 1949.

tanks. That same year, napalm was developed by Louis Fieser at Harvard. Napalm was a mixture of gasoline and palm oil thickeners. The thickeners turned the gas into jelly that stuck to the target as it burned. Napalm was efficient in burning large areas of foliage for a better view of the ground from the air. What wasn't documented publicly was that it also scorched the people it fell on.

Medical and Biological Advances

Not only did the war revolutionize weapons, it also jolted the healing professions into the modern era. Most important was the development and introduction of numerous antibiotics (anti-bacterial drugs), beginning with penicillin and sulfanilamide in 1940 and continuing with streptomycin in 1943, as well as many others. Anti-

biotics were miracle drugs; they killed infections — the sources of disease — outright. Few other drugs were able to do this; most treated symptoms alone. Now epidemic killers such as scarlet fever and tuberculosis could be cured. For doctors, as well as for patients of the forties, the idea that a disease could be killed off, not just alleviated, was a totally new idea. The war immediately proved antibiotics' value. Their use in military hospitals vastly reduced war-related fatalities and the spread of venereal diseases in the armed services. Indeed, military hospitals were at the forefront of such medical practices in the forties.

The military also found use for the new blood derivative called plasma, introduced in 1940. Plasma is the water-based medium of human blood, high in salt content, proteins, and chloride (much like the sea). It transports nutrients, maintains a stable body environment, and cleanses the internal organs. Plasma transfusions became widely used during the war, especially when whole blood was in short supply, as it was found to revive patients in shock or with severe hemorrhages from burns and trauma.

Advances in anesthesia — most notably the introduction of sodium pentothal and the creation of a specialized medical degree in anesthesiology — were also achieved in the decade. Prior to 1937, anesthesia consisted of an ether-soaked cloth held to the patient's face by a nurse. By 1940, almost one hundred doctors had been specifically trained to administer anesthesia and to monitor the patient's

vital functions during surgery. With the risk of infections reduced and controlled anesthesia available, more adventurous techniques in surgery were suddenly open to doctors, and the type of surgical operations broadened beyond the removal of tumors, limbs, and infected organs that had characterized surgery to that point.

Wider forays into surgery — particularly on the heart, lungs, and kidneys — brought about increasing specialization by doctors during the forties. Immediately following the war, the number of specializing physicians grew by 70 percent, largely because physicians were returning to private practice having learned the new techniques during the war. By decade's end, that number had more than doubled.

Among the decade's other notable medical developments, Sister Kenny introduced her famous therapy for infantile paralysis (poliomyelitis, or polio) victims in 1941, which employed the application of hot, moist packs to paralyzed muscles to soothe them and prevent deformities in children suffering from the disease. The epidemic was brought to an end when the polio virus was isolated in 1948 and the vaccine was invented by Dr. Jonas Salk in 1952.

Demerol, a synthetic morphine still widely used as a sedative-painkiller today, was developed in 1942 as was iodine therapy for thyroid malfunction. Anesthesia was introduced during childbirth in 1943, giving women a painless, though unconscious, way to deliver their babies. Cancer was first treated with radiation in 1948, bringing to fruition at least one utopian promise of nuclear science. Steroids, or synthetic hormones, were introduced in 1949

Sister Elizabeth Kenny greets lucky five-year-old Caroline Will, who was able to walk out of the hospital after only three months of treatment for infantile paralysis using the Kenny method.

and found to universally alleviate many different kinds of inflammation.

A rather ominous medical development of the decade was the discovery of radiation sickness in the Hiroshima and Nagasaki bomb survivors following the explosions and in the years that followed. Such intense radiation exposure had resulted in severe cell damage to tens of thousands of victims. They suffered acute cell death in their vital organs and genetic mutations that resulted in offspring with severe birth defects. Radiation sickness also resulted in infection, skin loss, cancer, nausea, vomiting, diarrhea, dehydration, sterility, and death.

The Social Sciences

In keeping with science's coldly rational stance in the nuclear age, the analysis of human relations became social science. A rational, scientific approach to human behavior would, it was hoped, yield a more rational people who had the ability to control the seemingly uncontrollable new products of science, such as atomic fission. And so, Americans went in search of moral certainties.

Nowhere was this rational approach more apparent than in the publication of *Sexual Behavior in the Human Male* in 1948 by Alfred C. Kinsey, followed in 1953 by *Sexual Behavior in the Human Female*. But Kinsey exploded any hope Americans may have had of moral certainties, at least where sex was concerned. Kinsey, with his partners Wardell B. Pomeroy and Clyde E. Martin, had undertaken in 1942 the first large-scale studies in history of human sexual behavior. This was no pop psychology book, but a scientific report by Kinsey's Institute for Sex Research, with support from Indiana University, the Rockefeller Foundation, and the National Research Council.

A zoologist by training, and a worldwide authority on wasps, Kinsey turned his keen observational powers on humans. He methodically questioned 5,300 white males and 5,490 white females about their sexual practices, including masturbation, premarital and extramarital intercourse, oral sex, and especially orgasm, which he called "outlets." Kinsey's aim was to "accumulate an objectively determined body of fact about sex which strictly avoids social or moral interpretations." His report revealed, for example, that 95 percent of American men had engaged in some sort of nonmarital, homosexual, or illegal sexual activity. Kinsey concluded that society's ideas of "normal and abnormal are seriously challenged."

Dr. Alfred Kinsey pioneered scientific research into the sexual habits of Americans. His research was published in 1948.

Dr. Benjamin McLane Spock. (1903-1998)

"Trust yourself. You know more than you think you do." In Baby and Child Care

Dr. Spock is best known as the author of The Common Sense Book of Baby and Child Care, a still much consulted book that he wrote while lieutenant commander in the navy in 1946. A Yale- and Columbia-trained pediatrician, Dr. Spock broke with years of child-rearing practice that had insisted on distant parental attitudes and inflexible feeding schedules. He recommended that parents be attentive to the individual child's needs and nature, and encouraged warm, loving relationships between parents and children.

His ideas had been formed partly in reaction to his mother's iron-willed child-rearing techniques with her own seven children, of which Benjamin was the eldest. Benny, as he was called, was a painfully shy and quiet person who had difficulty expressing himself to his disapproving mother. She refused to send her children to a regular school, having a governess tutor them instead. Not until age twelve was Benjamin Spock allowed to attend school with other boys his age. When he did, he felt that he'd been utterly liberated.

Spock's medical training and his marriage in 1927 to Jane Cheney took him away from the repressive home of his youth. During his training, he discovered a special affinity for children and decided to take a pediatric internship. In 1937, he did a year of psychiatric residency, primarily to help him discover ways "to bring up children without quite as many kinds of uneasiness as I had experienced," he explained in 1967.

As a young pediatrician, he held long consultations with patients and began to formulate a more relaxed approach to child rearing. Mothers were reassured that their natural instincts to love and nurture were on target, and found tremendous comfort in this reassurance.

At the urging of a paperback publisher who promised sales in the hundreds of thousands of copies, Dr. Spock began writing a book on parenting. In it, he took the innovative approach of linking physical and psychological events in childhood, and of viewing the child as a whole person with individual needs. His main aim was to increase parents' self-confidence and independence.

The public was highly receptive to his message, and the book became an instant bestseller, going into dozens of editions and foreign translations. Millions of copies sold. In a period of high conformity and growing Cold War sentiment, however, Dr. Spock was roundly accused of being much too permissive by many authorities in his field. Despite these critiques, Dr. Spock became a household word — the most trusted and influential authority on child rearing of the twentieth century.

Needless to say, the Kinsey report was criticized in the press and in the nation's pulpits for ignoring the emotional and moral side of human sexuality and for treating human behavior like animal behavior. Despite this, or because of its shock value, the books became immediate bestsellers. In fact, the Kinsey reports are still hailed as authoritative in the field and are credited with establishing sexology as a legitimate field of scientific inquiry.

American anthropologist Margaret Mead had first risen to fame after the 1928 publication of Coming of Age in Samoa, *and later,* Growing up in New Guinea, *where she investigated the social behavior of native children through adolescence. Using her knowledge of primitive cultures, she explored American cultural standards through her book,* Keep Your Powder Dry, *in 1942.*

The forties were years when national character studies became popular, arising from the the Cold War, and coloring even the most clinical-sounding social science with national self-interest. During the war, anthropologist Margaret Mead searched for characteristically American traits that would enable the U.S. to hold sway in the face of what appeared to be superior German,

Japanese, and Russian social uniformity and cohesiveness. In essence, she argued, in *Keep Your Powder Dry* (1942), that America's diversity and love of democracy were at the core of its strength. In *The American People* (1948), by Geoffrey Gorer, the author defined the American national character as having a feeling of superiority over other nations — as if the war had left any doubts in the American mind.

Women's Roles Defined

It was in the social sciences that the role of women was increasingly debated, with rather limiting consequences. Margaret Mead, who had done groundbreaking studies of adolescence in Samoan cultures during the twenties, had observed that Samoan female adolescent sexual behavior was strikingly open, and drew the then-shattering conclusion that female behavior is not biologically determined but learned from society. In *Male and Female* (1949), Mead flip-flopped, allowing that while limiting women's proper roles was wasteful of their other potential talents and even degrading, women's fulfillment of their biological roles would prevent the wasting of male talents, which, she insisted, naturally had a "razor-edge of extra gift . . . while women may easily follow where men lead, men will always make the new discoveries."

Mead's was just one of the many influential books of the time that sought to continue limiting women's roles. While American women had enjoyed their independence during the war, Freudian social scientists still insisted that women return to traditional roles in the home for everyone's general health and happiness. Helene Deutsch published *Psychology of Women* in 1944, openly criticizing career women and urging women to accept their predetermined role of biological motherhood, claiming to have found scientific evidence for her argument. Deutsch's book was the clinical basis for Marynia Farnham and Ferdinand Lundberg's *Modern Woman: The Lost Sex*, in which they argued that women who did not fulfill their traditional role were "truly displaced persons."

Technology in Everyday Life

Modern technology brought some startling new inventions into the home and into the lives of Americans. Some of these had profound consequences far into the late twentieth century. The most significant technological development was the transistor, developed at Bell Laboratories in New Jersey by John Bardeen and Walter Brattain in 1948.

The transistor was a tiny, highly portable, essential component of electrical circuit boards made of semiconducting materials. They could be used as amplifiers, detectors, or switches for electrical current. As such, they were extremely versatile, so much so that they entirely replaced vacuum tube technology and gave birth to the new field of solid-state electronics. Transistors were used in radios, TVs, phonographs, tape recorders, light dimmers, motors, watches, cameras, computers, guidance and surveillance systems, and myriad other things. Without transistors, the space age and the information age would have been impossible. For their work in this field, Bardeen and Brattain shared the Nobel Prize for Physics in 1956.

The first computer, the Mark I, was developed at Harvard University in 1942, in collaboration with IBM. ENIAC, the Electronic Numercial Integrator and Computer, was developed in 1946 at the University of Pennsylvania. These early computers were only capable of doing mathematics, though by the end of the decade, other applications were foreseen for computers, and the U.S. government wisely invested heavily in their development.

Computers could automatically perform complex calculations and process vast amounts of information in the blink of an eye. Though viewed as an oddity by many Americans in the early days, the computer's impact on human civilization came to be as profound as the discovery of fire, the development of the wheel, the harnessing of electricity, and the

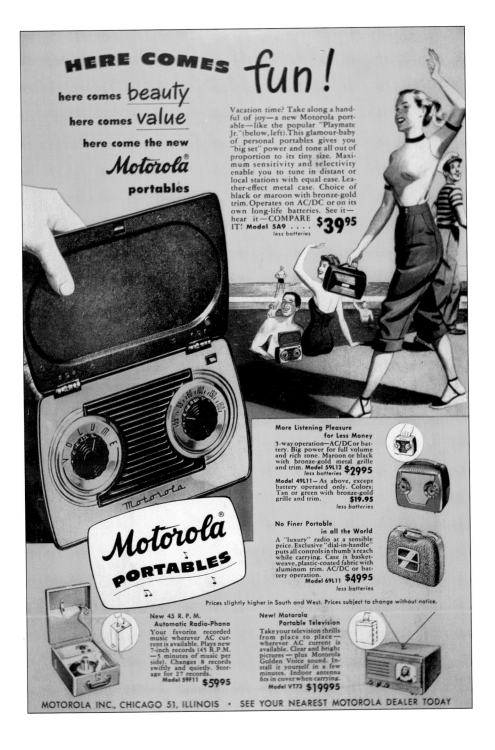

With the development of transistors, a lot of new "fun" products flooded the market to amuse and entertain Americans in their leisure hours, including televisions, radios, tape recorders, cameras, and phonographs.

Life was never to be the same once TV entered the home. As NBC president Niles Trammell announced in 1944, "Television promises to be the greatest medium of mass communication yet evolved." Though Roosevelt was the first president to appear on TV, it was Truman who first used the medium to address the nation. On October 5, 1947, he asked Americans to conserve food in order to aid the starving peoples of the world.

invention of the internal combustion engine. Today, even a simple bank deposit would be impossible without the all-knowing computer.

Perhaps the most ubiquitous technological innovation of the forties was the television. More than the computer, the TV rapidly changed American culture to the core. The technology for television had existed prior to the war but was not widespread, nor were there very many broadcasters. During the war, television's use had been limited and, indeed, curtailed by the Defense Communications Board for security reasons. Following the war, the U.S. television industry entered its first boom phase, setting up broadcast networks, manufacturing the actual units, and then selling them. The growth of the television industry during the late forties and fifties constituted the biggest mass media revolution seen since the introduction of the radio in the 1920s.

Almost immediately, television had a homogenizing effect on society.

With this new intruder in the living room came a new kind of social interaction that centered not on the people in the room but instead on the machine itself. This phenomenon resulted in an attempt by television manufacturers to advertise their product as a useful tool that inspired human interaction and physical activity. But the fact was, watching television did just the opposite.

Inventions for Everyday Life

The forties was also an era of developing high-tech gadgetry. Plastics came into their own during the forties, primarily as substitutes for wood, metal, and other natural resources that were scarce during the war. "Plastic," from the Greek *plastikos,* meaning "fit for molding," had been around since the late nineteenth century as celluloid, and its use had been limited to small personal items because it was highly flammable and turned brown when exposed to light.

In the forties, many new plastics were developed for a vast array of applications. The new plastics were totally synthetic, durable, and lightweight. They were used in buildings, light fixtures, car manufacturing, advertising, electrical installation, appliances, batteries, textiles, photography, packaging, sports, medicine, musical instruments (plastic bugles were even used in the army) and recordings, and even in aviation, shipping, and railways. Virtually everything that could possibly be made was suddenly being made from plastic.

A whole new field related to the chemistry, manufacture, and marketing of the stuff sprang up. One exam-

The ENIAC (Electronic Numerical Integrator and Calculator) computer was developed by J. P. Eckert and J. W. Mauchly of the University of Pennsylvania (shown center). It weighed thirty tons, contained eighteen thousand vacuum tubes, and was the size of a room. Modern desktop computers, by comparison, are much more powerful and faster, despite their compact size.

ple of new plastic was Teflon, first marketed by DuPont in 1948, which resisted adhesion to other surfaces. DuPont also introduced orlon and nylon, plastic-based fabrics, in the late thirties and forties as inexpensive substitutes for wool, cotton, and silk.

Photocopying was also developed in the late thirties and forties. The electrostatic copying process that used heat, light, and chemicals to reproduce black and white images had been invented by Chester Carlson in 1938. In 1947, Carlson sold the rights to his process to the Haloid Company, which coined the term "xerography" (from the Greek *xeros* for "dry" and *graphein* for "write") and changed the name of their company to the Xerox Corporation. Further development of the process was needed, and the first office copier was not sold until 1960, though its popularity was instantaneous and universal.

In 1947, the Polaroid Land camera was introduced to the market.

The first instant camera, it was both a camera and a darkroom in one. As if by magic, it developed, fixed, and printed the picture inside the body of the camera itself, within minutes. The revolutionary new camera was an instant success with thousands of the nation's shutterbugs.

In 1948, Peter Goldmark of Columbia Records developed the long-playing record, a plastic, grooved disk twelve inches in diameter. For decades, musical recordings had been capable of playing for no longer than five minutes at a stretch, first on wax, then later on plastic cylinders. The disk, with its closely spaced grooves etched into the plastic, could play up to twenty minutes per side on a phonograph with an needle-arm that rested in the grooves and transmitted the recording to the amplifier. It was the most popular recording format for more than forty years, until the development of compact laser disks in the 1980s.

Howard Hughes. (1905-1976)

Howard Robard Hughes is remembered for being one of the richest men in American history, dying with a personal fortune valued at over two billion dollars. He was a multifaceted, complex, and painfully reclusive individual, who managed to excel in several careers simultaneously.

Hughes was an indulged, overprotected only child who loved to build mechanical gadgets. His mother died when Howard was sixteen, and his father died three years later. Upon his death, Hughes inherited an estate worth $871,000 and his father's patent rights to a drill bit for gas and oil wells. The sale of these drill bits by the Hughes Tool Company formed the core of the Hughes fortune. By the time he was twenty, Hughes' annual income was $2 million.

But Hughes was not content to be just a tool manufacturer. With ample money to indulge his whims, Hughes became a movie producer and the owner of RKO Pictures, a movie studio, in the thirties. He discovered the young starlets Jean Harlow and Jane Russell and spared no expense promoting them and making them famous, first as classic pin-up girls, though Russell later proved herself an able actress.

Howard Hughes at the pilot's controls of his 200-ton flying boat, Spruce Goose, *in 1947.*

Hughes was not just a successful entrepreneur but also a gifted aviation engineer fascinated with flight. In the thirties, he broke several flight records, including one for speed in 1935, going 352 miles per hour. He also set an around-the-world flight record of three days, nineteen hours, and fourteen minutes. During the war, Hughes invested in aviation very seriously, forming the Hughes Aircraft Company and becoming one of the major U.S. defense contractors. The company developed many innovations in airplane technology and satellites, one of which was Hughes's own creation, the Lockheed Constellation, which became an important transcontinental shipping plane during the war. The Constellation also became the flagship of Trans World Airlines, of which Hughes owned most of the stock until 1966. Hughes also pushed for advanced instruments to be installed in planes and for greater use of ground navigation equipment.

Hughes himself designed and flew his own experimental aircraft. The most famous example of Hughes' inventiveness was the *HK-1 Hercules,* the so-called *Spruce Goose,* designed in 1947. This behemoth of a plane still holds the world's record for the largest wingspan of any airplane ever built, at 319 feet, 11 inches. It was made entirely of wood, had eight engines, and could hold seven hundred passengers. In 1947, Hughes himself piloted the *Spruce Goose* on its only flight. It flew one mile at a dizzying altitude of seventy feet and was the largest airplane in the world until the appearance of Boeing's 747 in the sixties. Today, this aeronautical oddity is displayed in Long Beach, California.

Toward the end of his life, Hughes became a total recluse, an eccentric seen by no one except a few trusted assistants. He died in flight from Mexico to Texas. Hughes's death was as surrounded by mystery as his life. Leaving no legally valid will, Howard Hughes's estate was claimed by several people, who produced wills allegedly signed by the billionaire, but these claims were never proven.

Another important recording technology was the German invention of reel-to-reel magnetic recording tape in 1942. Tape recordings were widely used during the war to fool the Allies; delayed broadcasts of Hitler's speeches made him appear to be in places he wasn't. After the war, the Ampex Corporation of California developed its own tape recording device based on the German model. The first delayed radio broadcast in the U.S. was the Bing Crosby Show in April, 1948, by the American Broadcasting Company.

In the huge field of food production, preparation, and preservation, a number of important breakthroughs occurred in tandem with the war demand. Insecticides and pesticides were widely introduced in the early forties, including DDT, to prevent crop damage and to raise the yield. The potato harvester, first used in 1941, sped up crop production. Freeze drying was first used in food preservation in 1940, while Bernard E. Proctor showed that irradiation of food was effective in maintaining freshness in 1943. After the war, freezers and frozen foods became commonplace. While the Tupperware Corporation, founded in 1945, developed plastic food storage containers, the Reynolds Metal Company introduced aluminum foil for home use in 1947.

Important Scientific Discoveries

One of the decade's most important scientific discoveries was the genetic role of DNA — deoxyribonucleic acid, the material in cells that contains the genetic code for living organisms — by Oswald Avery, Colin MacLeod, and Maclyn McCarty at the Rockefeller Institute in 1944. However, this information was virtually ignored by the scientific community, which at the time was searching for a link between physics and heredity rather than between biology and heredity. Here was further evidence of the powerful influence of the nuclear phenomenon on the framework of scientific thinking.

Other important genetic research was being done by Barbara McClintock, who showed in the forties that parts of genes could be rearranged to produce new genes, another finding that did not gain acceptance until the sixties. McClintock's groundbreaking discovery, unlike Oswald Avery's, was finally acknowledged with a Nobel Prize in 1983.

A less widely used but important discovery was the radiocarbon dating method in 1949, by Willard Frank Libby at the University of Chicago. This method of measuring the amounts of the radioactive isotope carbon 14 in substances to calculate their age was found to be extremely useful in dating objects of great antiquity. Anthropologists, archaeologists, and geologists could now accurately date material in the laboratory.

A novel and quite controversial theory of the origin of the universe, which has come to be called the Big Bang theory, was published by George Gamow in 1942, and later given great credibility by the nuclear explosions of 1945 through 1946. The Big Bang theory explained the origin of space and time as a powerful explosion of infinitely dense matter that expanded in a uniform, measurable way. Gamow's theory depended for its proof on Einstein's theory of relativity

Russian-born physicist George Gamow is credited as being among the first to propose the so-called Big Bang theory to explain the origins of the universe. He was also responsible for presenting some of the more complex aspects of modern science in a way that a lay audience could understand, through such books as Mr. Tompkins in Wonderland *(1939) and* Mr. Tompkins Explores the Atom *(1944).*

and the observable expansion and radiation in the universe. Many scientists up to the present have tried, with more and more convincing evidence, to prove the Big Bang theory, which is largely accepted in most scientific circles today as the explanation of the universe's beginnings.

This acceleration of scientific progress, made possible by huge sums of government money and the mind-altering changes of the advent of atomic energy, brought science into the modern age and laid the groundwork for the next phase: the space age of the fifties.

CHAPTER 7
The Arts and the Blossoming of Abstraction

American Art Goes International

Under Adolf Hitler, artists in Germany and in occupied lands quickly realized that any of their number who did not serve the Nazis' political purposes would be wiped out just as the religious, scientific, and intellectual communities had been. Droves of European artists in every field — literature, music, theater, dance, and the visual arts — fled to the U.S. in the late thirties and early forties. Most settled in New York City, instantly making it the world's center of artistic creativity. Walter Cook, then head of the Institute of Fine Arts at New York University said, "Hitler shook the trees, and I picked up the apples."

This artistic immigration had an immediate and profound effect on American art. Where American artists of the thirties had emphasized folklore and regional subjects and created highly realistic art, in the forties they abandoned this style for entirely different techniques. For one thing, the presence of so many new talents from Europe brought new styles and ideas that American artists wished to try. For another, the war had raised moral questions that artists wished to answer through their art. Thus American artists left off painting cityscapes and the like, as both American and visiting European artists moved away from painting subjects altogether. Art became more and more abstract, as artists tried daring new techniques, asked new questions, and found bold new answers. The resulting impact on the art world was startling.

Chaos on Canvas

It is perhaps foolish to generalize about artists as a group because they work alone and each has a highly individual style. But it is safe to draw a few conclusions about the artists of the forties. Before and during the war, many modern artists explored ancient myths and used psychological theories to create abstract art. After 1945, the atom bomb and all its consequences had an even greater effect on art.

Arshile Gorky's Virginia Landscape *(1943). Gorky was one of the leading abstractionists of the early forties, known for his fluid painting style. He enjoyed a number of exhibitions in his lifetime and in 1946 was represented at the "Fourteen Americans" show at the Museum of Modern Art in New York City.*

The bomb had obliterated cities, but it had also expanded a way of seeing life. The future had become an uncertain thing. Artists picked up on this idea of fundamental change, and the art they created was just as explosive as the bomb. Artists rejected every artistic tradition that had gone before, searching for a way to express themselves that was completely new.

Popular culture — magazines, radio, movies, and the like — was quick to use positive atomic images, and the public was quick to adopt them. Fine artists, however, saw the bomb as a symbol of obliteration and nothingness — and this is what they painted, danced, or composed. Abstract art bore no resemblance to anything anyone had ever seen or imagined; it was shocking — deliberately so. It was nothing but color, form, texture, or shape. Abstract art, in short, embodied the chaos of modern times. It was a way for artists to say that historical progress was not meaningful, good, or even possible.

In an era of rising anticommunism and HUAC inquiries in Hollywood, abstract art was also a way of commenting on the state of the world without taking an openly political stance: Who could detect an artist's political views from blobs of black paint? By being utterly baffling, abstract art was a safe way for artists to say something new and unpopular in a highly conformist age. The painter Robert Motherwell summed it up in November, 1944, when he said, "The artist has had to replace other social values with the strictly aesthetic." That is, he believed it was no longer possible for art to have a message; art had to rely strictly on its looks.

Abstract Expressionism

In the visual arts, chaos was most quickly adopted as a theme. Old traditions were swept away, and painters "pulverized," as painter Mark Rothko put it, "the familiar identity of things." Rothko, together with such painters as Jackson Pollock, Willem de Kooning, Robert Motherwell, Lee Krasner, Franz Kline, Piet Mondrian, Arshile Gorky, and Adolf Gottleib became a loose association of artists called the abstract expressionists. This group completely changed painting. There were no recognizable objects in their works, no stories — just color, texture, and form. Some even rejected the use of frames, and the very idea of composing a painting to fit the canvas was thrown out. They made enormous canvases, far too big for a traditional living room. Painters such as Pollock and Rothko even gave their paintings numbers rather than names, removing yet another point of reference for the viewer to relate to.

Yellow, Grey, Black (1948), by Jackson Pollock is typical of the chaos of color and form embraced by the new abstract expressionists.

Individual self-expression was the main concern of the expressionists, hence their name. The process of making a painting replaced subject matter as the source of artistic exploration. Indeed, since subject matter was deemed irrelevant, process was elevated to a new level of importance. The random, the surreal, and the unconscious were explored for their visual effects. The painters who produced these works came to be known as "action painters," in which the act of an artist working with materials took precedence over the finished product.

Calder's Mobiles

Abstraction, though seemingly chaotic and random, also had its craft. To achieve spectacular new effects in sculpture, for instance, great skill was required to get that "apparent accident," as sculptor Alexander Calder put it. Causing a revolution similar to Pollock's in painting, Calder forever changed sculpture with the deceptively simple concept of random movement within his creations.

Calder created mobiles, objects that were attached to one another and carefully balanced to move in space according to environmental conditions. It was not just spontaneous movement that interested Calder, but also the "changing relationship of the parts to each other," writes Matthew Baigell. Calder was, says Baigell, "the first to allow process and chance to alter the forms of his pieces. No other American had yet contributed so fundamentally to the progress of modern art."

In stationary sculpture, traditional materials such as bronze and marble were being swapped for steel and so-called found objects. The most innovative sculptors in this field were David Smith, Joseph Cornell, and Isamu Noguchi. These sculptors rendered living forms in abstract ways, giving them a primitive (that is, untaught) quality, almost like a totem.

Abstract Architecture

Architecture also experienced major changes during the forties, much of it due to European émigré influence. It, too, became more abstract and anonymous. In the late forties, émigré Ludwig Mies Van Der Rohe popularized the glass-curtain skyscraper that became much imitated in many American cities. The building style was futuristic, indeed, but ultimately sterile in feel.

In 1943, Frank Lloyd Wright had begun designing the Solomon R. Guggenheim Museum in New York City, his last significant building. A tortuously complex project for the architect, it was the butt of many jokes. Critics called it "the snail," "an indigestible hot cross bun," "a washing machine," and "an inverted oatmeal dish." Yet it was the culmination of Wright's entire career — the embodiment of all his architectural principles. Completed in 1959, it was (and still is) the world's only upwardly and outwardly spiraling building.

Modern Dance Innovations

The performing arts also underwent a transformation. In dance, the most revolutionary influence was Martha Graham, who blossomed into a mature artist in the forties. Graham's

"We are freeing ourselves of the impediments of memory, association, nostalgia, legend, myth, or what have you, that have been the devices of Western European painting."

Abstract expressionist painter Barnett Newman

Agnes De Mille. (1905-1993)

Agnes De Mille was one of the forties' most creative popular choreographers; her style changed both American ballet and the Broadway musical, fields in which she was equally productive. De Mille's style was theatrical and broad, her classical training imbued with an interest in communicating personality through body language. Combining an eclectic mix of American folk dancing, classical ballet, and informal gesture, De Mille captured the way Americans saw themselves ideally: buoyant, happy, sentimental, and optimistic. De Mille's choreography wove a dramatic thread with movement, and she rejected the abstractions of Martha Graham and Merce Cunningham, though she was one of the first choreographers to work for both classical and modern dance companies. A woman of the times, she was an ardent patriot and preferred American themes in her dances.

Born in 1905 to theatrical parents and niece of film director Cecil B. De Mille, Agnes De Mille grew up in the theater and surrounded by theater people. By 1914, she decided to become a dancer and followed this dream despite her father's disapproval, making her New York debut in a 1928 production of *Stage Fright*. Throughout the thirties, De Mille choreographed for European dance troupes, Hollywood movies, and the American Ballet Theater in New York.

In 1942, De Mille's first major success was the ballet *Rodeo*, a story about western ranch life, set to Aaron Copland's music. *Rodeo* was the first real evidence that American subjects could be treated classically.

De Mille's biggest success came in 1943, with the Broadway musical *Oklahoma!* With music and lyrics by Richard Rodgers and Oscar Hammerstein II, it was the story of a pair of rural lovers and the farm hand who tries to come between them; it was an American story to the core. De Mille's contribution wasn't merely to provide a spectacle — her dances helped tell the story to a degree never done before. What's more, her dancers had to really act their parts in character. These techniques made a lasting impact on Broadway choreography.

With her career thus firmly established, Agnes De Mille went on to choreograph other Broadway hits, notably *Carousel* (1945), *Brigadoon* (1947), for which she won the Tony Award, and *Gentlemen Prefer Blondes* (1949). Her ballets of the period included *Tally-Ho* (1944) and *Fall River Legend* (1948).

In her later years, she continued to choreograph and became a spokesperson and lecturer, who championed federal support for the arts. During a gala in 1990, De Mille gave her definition of American dance: "Ours is an up beat, a hurried, hasty beat. It keeps pressing us to go farther, to include everything so that we can savor everything, so that we can know everything, so that we will miss nothing. Partly it's greed, but mainly it's curiosity. We just want to experience it. And we do." She died of a stroke at the age of eighty-eight.

Agnes De Mille (right) shows Norma Shearer the steps of an Italian Renaissance waltz.

Merce Cunningham is
credited with redefining and
evolving a new vocabulary
for modern dance.
Appearing with the Martha
Graham Dance Company
from 1939 to 1945, he
began choreographing
himself in 1942 and
performed his first solo
concert with composer John
Cage in 1944. This
composite photograph shows
Cunningham performing
Root of Unfocus
in that same year.

subjects up to 1945 were studiedly American, but, in the late forties, she turned to mythological subjects. Yet Graham took a different tack with narrative dance. She abandoned the style, which was so heavy with acting, for an entirely new way of communicating with motion, creating a language of the body. Developing a technique of strict physical discipline, Graham used form, repetition, and variation of pattern to tell her story. Usually, however, there was still some vestige of a story. Her hallmark choreography to Aaron Copland's *Appalachian Spring* in 1944, for example, interpreted a love story in modern movements.

Graham's student and a member of her troupe, Merce Cunningham, took the Graham technique one step further. Cunningham abandoned the story altogether. Mood, emotion, and form were to him what color, texture, and shape were to painter Jackson Pollock — the means for self-expression to achieve even greater abstraction in dance. Cunningham sought a marriage of pure movement with music. In fact, his early collaboration in 1944, with composer John Cage, an early proponent of atonal, dissonant sound, merged sound and nonnarrative movement into something never before experienced as dance.

Theater Enjoys an Audience

Abstraction extended its influence to the theater, too. The most abstract, and indeed bizarre, play of the decade was Thornton Wilder's *The Skin of Our Teeth,* which opened in November 1942. Wilder's play was a family saga that began in the Ice Age and progressed to the future, containing bizarre juxtapositions and humorous anachronisms that many found hard to understand. Yet Wilder's play was an instant hit and ran for forty-five weeks, winning the Pulitzer Prize. It remains a popular revival play to this day.

"The lift of the arm does not mean that it represents a tree or anything else. The arm raised in an uplift that is graceful presents the beauty of an arm in motion. It is enough. America is not interested in impressionism. Our dramatic force lies in energy and vitality."

Martha Graham

"Tennessee" Williams. (1911-1983)

Thomas Lanier "Tennessee" Williams was one of the most prolific dramatists in American twentieth-century literary history and also one of the most compelling. He was the author of thirty full-length plays, thirty-five short plays, two volumes of poetry, two novels, one book of essays, and his own memoirs. Fifteen of his plays were made into films, and two served as operatic librettos. Throughout his long though uneven career, Williams persevered as a writer, despite the mixed reception to his various works.

Born in Columbus, Mississippi, Williams mined to great effect the southern way of speaking, and explored complex family relationships and personal agonies in his plays. Themes of sexual frustration, suppressed violence, and inner torment are common throughout his work.

Much of his writing is autobiographical. He grew up in the home of his maternal grandfather, an Episcopal minister, until he and his mother and father moved to St. Louis in 1918, after which his family disintegrated. He began to write in 1922. Young Williams hopped from factory job to shoe salesman, and from college to college, finally graduating from the University of Iowa in 1938.

In 1939, Williams officially changed his first name to Tennessee, after his father's home state. Under this name, he won a play writing contest. *The Battle of Angels* opened in 1940 off-Broadway, but its sexual and religious content offended audiences, so the play closed after only a few performances. In 1957, Williams revised the play and produced it as *Orpheus Descending,* which became the movie *The Fugitive Kind* in 1960. This is but one of many examples in which Williams revised, reworked, or entirely rewrote earlier material for later productions. From 1940 to 1945, Williams also made a living as a scriptwriter for MGM studios.

Williams had *The Glass Menagerie*, his first major play, produced in 1945. Like most of his work, this play featured self-deluded characters in search of fulfillment. Its raw and open emotionalism drew a following, and Williams' dramatic reputation was established. He followed this with his most fully realized play, *A Streetcar Named Desire,* in 1947, which was made into a film in 1951. It featured the once-genteel Blanche DuBois, caught in a helpless spiral of despair and madness as she tries to survive hostile realities of modern life, represented by her brutish brother-in-law, Stanley Kowalski. With this play, Williams was universally hailed as the finest dramatist of the postwar era, and the play won the Pulitzer Prize.

Williams' other major plays included *Summer and Smoke* (1948), *The Rose Tattoo* (1951), *Cat on a Hot Tin Roof* (1955), which also won a Pulitzer, and *Night of the Iguana* (1961). Williams' career was interrupted periodically by his continuing addiction to drugs and alcohol, and by his problems with depression. In 1969, he suffered a complete breakdown, though he recovered and continued to write until his death.

Wilder was the most innovative playwright of the decade, though there were other great American playwrights working during the forties in a more traditional vein. These included Tennessee Williams (*The Glass Menagerie,* 1945; *A Streetcar Named Desire,* 1947); Arthur Miller (*All My Sons,* 1947); Lillian Hellman (*The Watch on the Rhine,* 1941, and *Another Part of the Forest,* 1946); and Eugene O'Neill (*The Iceman Cometh,* 1946).

With scenes that would have made audiences blush just twenty years before, A Streetcar Named Desire, Tennessee Williams' hard-hitting 1947 drama, was set in a sweltering New Orleans slum. Here we see Kim Hunter, Jessica Tandy, and Marlon Brando in the stage version of the play that was to help Brando on the road to stardom when it was released as a movie in 1951.

These American masters of drama relied more heavily on traditional structure than Wilder, but brought to their plays an increasing level of shock value and a psychological intensity typical of the new genre.

Theater, both dramatic and musical, enjoyed an astonishing number of openings and long runs during the forties, despite war's interruptions. Musical talents such as Richard Rodgers and Oscar Hammerstein II,

Allan Jay Lerner, and Irving Berlin produced some of their best work in this period. Audiences flocked to the theater in huge numbers. Many of these plays became classics of the American theater, such as *Pal Joey* (1940), *Arsenic and Old Lace* (1941), *Oklahoma!* (1943), *Carousel* (1945), and *Annie Get Your Gun* (1946), just to name a few. The decade was a golden age of Broadway musicals.

Out of popular Broadway musicals emerged some of America's favorite songs. From the smash hit *Oklahoma!* in 1943 came no fewer than eight hit songs, including "Oh, What a Beautiful Mornin'," "Oklahoma!," "People Will Say We're in Love," and "The Surrey with the Fringe on Top." Broadway's great musical master, Irving Berlin, also contributed "How I Hate to Get Up in the Morning" for *This Is the Army* (1942), the only Broadway play ever to have had a cast made up entirely of soldiers, "There's No Business Like Show Business," and "The Girl That I Marry" from *Annie Get Your Gun*.

Musical Richness

The American musical scene of the forties was marked by a wide diversity of classical, popular, and jazz styles. Classical music was especially energized by many European émigré composers and conductors. These immigrants included Bruno Walter, George Szell, Bela Bartok, Arnold Schoenberg, Paul Hindemith, Kurt Weill, and Nadia Boulanger. Many of these introduced a more abstract, less melodious, music to American ears.

But native-born American composers of the forties did not completely succumb to the European sound. In fact, traditional American themes and sounds were patriotically the order of the day. Aaron Copland incorporated folksy Shaker tunes in *Appalachian Spring* (1944), and wrote the all-American ballets, *Billy the Kid* (1938) and *Rodeo* (1942). Samuel Barber revived the marching band tempo in *Commando March* (1943), while upholding the romantic tradition. Other American musicians of note were Jerome Kern and Leonard Bernstein (who made his conducting debut in 1948), who also used solidly American sounding themes.

In the area of composition, John Cage was the most revolutionary musician of the decade. Cage, inspired by the work of European Arnold Schoenberg, dancer Merce Cunningham, and sculptor Alexander Calder, took the idea of randomness and applied it to musical composition, rejecting melody altogether. Cage's music was antimusic. He experimented with time, chance occurrence, and silence, and sought disharmony and difference rather than predictability, using, for example, twelve radios at once to produce *Imaginary Landscape No. 4* (1951). His music did not appeal to a wide popular audience, but his experimentation produced the most unusual music of that — or indeed of any — decade.

Popular Music's Heyday

In popular music, the era of the early forties was the heyday of the big band. This music had wide appeal to white audiences because it was so danceable and upbeat. Big bands — so called because they were composed of dozens of musicians and orchestrated by a bandleader — were a public display for musicians and audiences alike of America's team spirit for the war effort. Bandleaders, such as Glenn Miller, Harry James, Tommy Dorsey, Duke Ellington, Benny Goodman, Stan Kenton, and Lionel Hampton, provided catchy, carefully orchestrated sounds for the widest possible audiences. Glen Miller's "Chattanooga Choo Choo" (1941) and "String of Pearls" (1942) are but two famous examples of big popular band arrangements.

Naturally, music could be a great morale lifter during wartime. Patriotic songs abounded, such as "G.I. Jive," "Rosie the Riveter," "Praise the Lord and Pass the Ammunition," and "This is the Army, Mr. Jones." Throughout the war, Kate Smith sold war bonds and belted out her hit "God Bless America" (1938). The Andrews Sisters, touring with the USO (United Service Organization), rendered uplifting and complicated three-part harmonies in such hits as "Don't Sit Under the Apple Tree" (1942) and "Boogie Woogie Bugle Boy of Company B" (1943).

"It was like everybody in the United States held on to each other's hands. I felt we were invincible. Right is right and we were right and we're gonna win."

Maxene Andrews, one of the singing Andrews Sisters, quoted in *The Good War* by Studs Terkel

Glenn Miller supposedly earned the money for his first trombone by milking cows near his Iowa home. By the 1940s, the Glenn Miller Orchestra was touring the country, riding the crest of the big band wave. His first successful recording as a bandleader was "In the Mood," in 1939. He died tragically in a plane crash in Europe in 1944. Here, he and the band play during a hotel date broadcast during the early forties.

"Kate" Smith. (1909-1986)

Kathryn "Kate" Elizabeth Smith was an American institution virtually from the moment she first opened her mouth and sang on the radio in 1930. For fifty years, Smith's wide, smiling face and unmistakable voice were everywhere on radio and television. In her career, she recorded three thousand songs, a thousand of which were original — more songs than recorded by any other popular singer. For years, she was perennially among the most admired women in America.

As a child entertainer, she sang to American troops during World War I. Determined that their daughter would amount to something, her parents sent her to nursing school, which she quit in 1926 to sing with the Eddie Dowling Revue. Throughout the late twenties, Kate Smith was a vaudeville performer.

At the age of twenty-two, Smith made her CBS radio debut in 1930, singing "When the Moon Comes Over the Mountain." She was an instant hit, and the song became her theme. She hosted her own radio show, "Kate Smith Speaks," throughout the thirties. In 1938, Kate Smith became an American icon with her recording of Irving Berlin's "God Bless America." The song remained an enormous hit throughout the patriotically tinted war years, and Kate Smith became the symbol of American patriotism.

Along with her male equivalent, Arthur Godfrey, Smith was one of the most popular hosts in commercial radio of the early forties. Her voice was a loud, almost hearty bellow, which grabbed attention. To this she added charisma and a folksy image that came across as totally sincere. This made her an unequaled spokesperson for any product she chose to sell, even though she made an average of six new commercials each week. She insisted on trying every product before she sold it. In an era when listeners were bombarded by advertising for everything under the sun, Americans trusted her. A public poll taken of Kate Smith fans in 1945 found her most attractive traits were her sincerity, her philanthropy, her patriotism, and her down-to-earth quality. To many of her admirers, she had a heart of gold.

It was Americans' faith in Kate Smith — and their adoration of her — that helped her become the nation's premier war bond salesperson during the early forties. Here again, her sincerity, coupled with the urgency of the cause, helped her raise $39 million in a one-day, marathon radio war-bond drive. It did not hurt her cause that Smith refused payment for these marathon bond sales. Lack of self-interest only endeared her more to her listeners. If she could put herself through eighteen hours of work for no pay, then she had surely earned the moral authority to sell a patriotic item like a war bond.

In the fifties and sixties, Smith continued to host radio and television programs and to sing, though her style became dated. Her health began to fail in the seventies, and in 1986, she died.

Harry "Bing" Crosby. (1904-1977)

Bing Crosby was one of the most listened-to singers of the forties and perhaps of all time. Crosby's trademark was his rich, smooth voice and versatile phrasing; he made melodies flow with incredible ease. He exuded sincerity and an easygoing charm; he made his work look effortless. Crosby was a sentimental crooner, yet his repertoire was broad, going from fast-paced jazz numbers to lilting love ballads.

Bing Crosby had one of the most varied, most successful, and longest careers in show business. Born in Tacoma, Washington, he attended Gonzaga University, leaving before graduation to become a vocalist with Paul Whiteman and the Rhythm Boys. Between 1930 and 1949, Bing Crosby became the hottest-selling singer in the radio industry, a superstar. His records appeared on the charts 340 times and forty of them reached number one. By the time of his death, he had sold more than 300 million records in America and one billion worldwide! At the peak of his career, Crosby was appearing in three movies per year, hosting a one-hour radio program, making recordings, and making frequent guest appearances. During the war, he added to these activities by going to war bond rallies, a job that he said had been the most rewarding of his total career. All this acclaim came to Crosby, despite the fact that he rarely performed for a live audience after 1932.

Beginning in the thirties, Crosby also appeared in short, one-reel musical comedies. Few popular singers had ever gone successfully from radio to movies, but Hollywood spotted a gold mine in Crosby's debonair, yet self-effacing manner. A feature film actor during the forties, Crosby became one of Hollywood's top ten box office stars for more than twenty years — he was number one from 1944 through 1949 — and was the first popular singer ever to win an Academy Award.

Crosby's movies were mainly musicals, capitalizing on his velvet voice. In 1942, he recorded "White Christmas," a sentimental ballad that brought tears to the eyes of many a soldier overseas. The song became an instant classic, particularly after Crosby appeared in *Holiday Inn* with Fred Astaire in 1942, in which he sang not just this hit, but also "Easter Parade." Crosby's movie career got its biggest boost in 1943, when he starred in *Going My Way*, in which he sang "Silent Night."

In the forties, Crosby also became famous for the so-called Road pictures in which he teamed up with comedian Bob Hope and actress Dorothy Lamour. This was a series of zany, madcap, and, for the most part, utterly improbable comedies that included *Road to Singapore* (1940), *Road to Zanzibar* (1941), *Road to Morocco* (1942), *Road to Utopia* (1945), and *Road to Rio* (1947), for a total of seven Road movies between 1940 and 1962.

Crosby's boy-next-door image masked a troubled family life. He worked constantly, and was rarely at home with his wife and four sons. Behind the charming facade he projected to the public, he was a chronic alcoholic with a violent temper. Crosby is remembered with fear by his grown children. When he was at home, he was a stern disciplinarian who meted out physical punishments with a strap. Hiding his and his first wife's drinking from the public (she died of cancer in 1952), Crosby appeared to embody the ideal American family man. He did not stop drinking until late in his life.

Bing Crosby (left) and Bob Hope do the highland fling in one of their many joint movies, Road to Bali.

Frank Sinatra's boyish yet sophisticated good looks, and easy velvet voice earned him the reputation of the world's most popular crooner.

Outnumbering these gung-ho songs, however, were a great many sentimental ones, full of nostalgia and anxiety over separation, such as "As Time Goes By," "I'll Be Seeing You," "I'm Making Believe," "I'll Remember April," "We'll Meet Again," and "You'd Be So Nice to Come Home To." These songs reflected the yearning for peace, stability, and home that was at the root of America's push toward victory.

In popular music, Bing Crosby was hands down the most listened-to artist of the decade. But the sentimental croonings of Frank Sinatra gave rise to fan hysteria never before seen in America. Sinatra's early years in Harry James's big band began his long career in which he perfected an openly sensual singing style and seductive voice in such hits as "All or Nothing at All" and "I Couldn't Sleep a Wink Last Night." Sinatra's youthful good looks, his suave manner, and his gorgeous voice all combined to make him one of the most popular singers of the decade. Even Bing Crosby, the smooth-toned boy next door, whose international hit record of 1942, "White Christmas," became an instant classic with record-breaking sales, could not claim such abject devotion from his many fans.

Bebop and Rhythm and Blues

Supplanting the homogenized sound of the big bands by 1948 was bebop jazz. A singularly black musical expression, it drew on African musical influences, yet was a new form based on the African-American experience, rebellious and defiant of white culture. Bebop was fast, spontaneous, intricate, improvised, and irregular, and its high priest was saxophonist Charlie Parker. Other bebop artists of note were Dizzy Gillespie, Max Roach, Thelonious Monk, Miles Davis, and Woody Herman.

Another new jazz form called rhythm and blues was also born in the late forties, a step beyond the rural-based blues that had arisen in the early twentieth century. R & B was urban music with gospel roots, a reflection of African-American migration from

Charlie "Bird" Parker, with Dizzie Gillespie and John Coltrane in 1950. With Gillespie, drummer Kenny Clarke, and pianist Thelonious Monk, he performed in jam sessions at Minton's Play House where bebop was founded. Parker made records with Gillespie in 1945, notably "Hot House" and "Salt Peanuts," which made him the leading exponent of bebop.

Billie Holiday. (1915-1959)

Born Eleanora Fagan, the daughter of a roving guitarist, young Billie Holiday first heard the jazz recordings of Louis Armstrong and Bessie Smith at a brothel where she ran errands for the madam. As a young woman, Holiday was a prostitute but soon followed her dream of becoming a professional singer by moving to Harlem in 1931 and singing in nightclubs there, making her first record in 1933.

Her first big success came in 1935. She toured in the late thirties with the bands of Count Basie and Artie Shaw. In 1940, Billie Holiday came into her own as a solo nightclub star, singing her richly nuanced and melancholy songs to rapt audiences. Considered the finest female jazz singer of her time — and probably of any time — Holiday used her untrained yet magnificent voice to create previously unheard effects, tones, and phrasings. She brought to her delivery a deep sense of personal sorrow that rendered even the simplest lyrics memorable.

From 1936 to 1943, Holiday's private and professional relationship with jazz saxophonist Lester Young broke new ground in music, as voice and instrument seemed to talk to each other. Young nicknamed her "Lady Day," a name that stuck. Some of Holiday's most memorable songs were "Lady Sings the Blues," "Strange Fruit," and "Do Nothing, Til You Hear from Me." Most of her songs dealt with a loss of love, frustrated passion, and unhappy relationships with men.

Holiday's late years were a tragic downward spiral of abusive relationships and the heroin addiction that eventually killed her. Her jewel-clear voice was destroyed by the drugs, though she continued to sing with great technique and emotion. Her autobiography, *Lady Sings the Blues,* written with W. Dufty, was published in 1956, and a movie based on the book was produced in 1972.

rural to urban settings. Playing in R & B clubs in Memphis, Kansas City, Philadelphia, and elsewhere, black musicians brought their soulful, heartfelt rhythms and themes of love and loss to large white audiences and into the mainstream for the first time. In fact, R & B's popularity caused *Billboard* magazine to change its name from "race music" to "rhythm and blues" in 1949.

Black female R & B vocalists set the standard for jazz singing. The emotion-laden phrasing of Billie Holiday, the cool sophistication of Sarah Vaughan, and the wildly improvisational scat of Ella Fitzgerald were art forms in themselves. These women were just a lucky few who attained fame in this medium, despite a large number of aspiring male artists with an equally rich repertoire. Black male R & B soloists and groups never attained the commercial success of their female counterparts because white-owned studios were reluctant to give them recording contracts, and when they did, they were paid much less than whites. Nevertheless, the studios capitalized on their black talent,

hiring white groups to record black R & B songs, using the argument that the white version would sell better. Later, white musicians such as Jerry Lee Lewis and Elvis Presley borrowed (and some would argue, stole) from rhythm and blues to invent rock 'n' roll in the following decade.

A Literary Plateau

The forties were not a time of robust literary innovation such as had characterized the twenties and thirties. The stylistic inventions of William Faulkner, Ernest Hemingway, and T. S. Eliot had been largely absorbed. The experimentation that was going on at this time in the other arts had actually occurred much earlier in American literature.

The war, while providing writers with much fresh material, did not significantly change American writers' stylistic approach, though it did give rise to the reportorial novel. The most famous of these were John Hersey's *A Bell for Adano* (1944) and his *Hiroshima*

(1946), Irwin Shaw's *The Young Lions* (1948), and Norman Mailer's *The Naked and the Dead* (1948), all realistic war novels of the most somber sort. But war was largely a subject of nonfiction titles, the most notable of which were by eyewitnesses to the event, such as William Shirer's *Berlin Diary* (1941) and *The Rise and Fall of the Third Reich* (1950), reporter Ernie Pyle's *Here is Your War* (1943) and *Brave Men* (1944), Captain Ted Lawson's *Thirty Seconds Over Tokyo* (1943), and Richard Tregaskis's *Guadalcanal Diary* (1943), among many others. Literally dozens of war books rode the bestseller lists in the forties; war was largely a popular subject for a wide audience. Even comic books reflected this, as evidenced by the huge popularity of square-jawed World War II comic book soldier Steve Canyon.

The lessons of the Cold War did not go unabsorbed by writers, however. Political absolutes gave rise to moral absolutism in the hard-boiled detective works of Mickey Spillane. Spillane's Mike Hammer was a man's man, a war veteran turned private eye, who, beginning with *I, The Jury* in 1947, dispatched an endless array of thugs, punks, and villains with moral righteousness backed with plain old physical violence. Might equalled right, and America was always right.

Regionalism crept into the literature, including Robert Penn Warren's *All the King's Men* (1946), Truman Capote's *Other Voices, Other Rooms* (1948), Carson McCullers' *The Heart Is a Lonely Hunter* (1940) and *Member of the Wedding* (1946), and Eudora Welty's *Delta Wedding* (1946), all of which described the South. William Saroyan's *The Human Comedy* (1943), was set in small town California. Richard Wright, with *Native Son*

(Left) "The First Lady of Song" Ella Fitzgerald, achieved national fame after the 1938 release of "A-Tisket, A-Tasket," which she cowrote with bandleader Chick Webb. After Webb's death, she took over his band before becoming a highly successful solo performer. Her repertoire ranges from popular ballads to calypso, blues, and Dixieland, and her most popular albums are those featuring songs by Cole Porter, George Gershwin, Irving Berlin, and Richard Rodgers and Lorenz Hart.

Richard Nathaniel Wright. (1908-1960)

Born in Natchez, Mississippi, to a childhood of severe poverty and neglect, Richard Wright watched his mother become paralyzed and spent part of his childhood in an orphanage. Wright left home at age fifteen to fend for himself, having witnessed the lynching of a step-uncle and a friend. Joining the growing ranks of African-Americans migrating north, Wright made his way to Memphis, Tennessee, where his first exposure to good books made him decide to become a writer. Roaming the country and doing odd jobs, Wright settled in Chicago in 1934 and became active in the Communist party. He would later regret this alliance for personal and patriotic reasons.

In 1937, Wright was employed by the Works Progress Administration in the Federal Writers' Project in New York, his first real opportunity to be a professional writer. But Wright's first major success, and the one for which he is best remembered, came in 1940, when he was awarded a Guggenheim Fellowship. The money gave him the time he needed to finish writing his novel, *Native Son,* which was published that year. The book drew instant acclaim from both black and white audiences, unusual for a black author of the time. Its plot revolved around a young black Chicagoan named Bigger Thomas, a man convicted of murder, whom Wright portrayed sympathetically as the victim of social injustice. In 1941, a Broadway play based on *Native Son* was produced, though by the blockbuster standards of the day, it had a fairly short run of less than a year.

In 1945, Wright scored a second success with *Black Boy,* an autobiography of his miserable childhood in the South, which is considered to be his major literary achievement. In all of his work, Wright championed the African-American cause in strident, angry tones. It was this sense of urgency as well as the content of his message, that helped him gain the public eye. But as many other black civil rights advocates of the day were discovering, their efforts to achieve racial equality were most unwelcome to the U.S. government. Almost any attempts to remedy racial discrimination were regarded as equivalent to sedition.

In Wright's case, his civil rights stance was further complicated by his open involvement in the Communist party. This, compounded with his race, made him a ripe target. He came under surveillance by the FBI as early as 1940, was suspected of subversion, and in 1944, was publicly denounced as a Communist. Ironically, throughout Wright's tenure as a party member, he had chafed under Communist-style authority and officially left the party in 1945.

But his persecution continued. In 1947, seeking relief from pressure by the FBI and the CIA to inform on his former Communist comrades, Wright and his wife and daughter moved to Paris in a self-imposed exile. But although Paris was a less racist environment for Wright, the government harassment continued, particularly as the State Department threatened to rescind his passport. He died of a heart attack, which many of his friends blamed on the stress and anxiety he suffered at the hands of the government.

Wright, however, had established himself not just as an important black writer, but also as a successful writer in general. His books were translated into dozens of languages, and until his sudden death, he remained the most famous African-American writer in America.

(1940) and *Black Boy* (1945), was the first black writer to find a wide popular white audience in America.

The variety and quality of American literature in the forties, both popular and critically acclaimed, fiction and non-fiction, was high. But there could be little doubt that American writers had gone through an evolutionary change in the previous twenty years and were assimilating these changes in preparation for the next major movement in American letters: the Beat Generation of the fifties.

CHAPTER 8
The Golden Age of Media

War, the Lead Story

The movies, radio, and journalism were all affected by the fight to liberate Europe and the Pacific. The war's events made people hungrier for news than they had ever been, and a boom in radio news programs, movie newsreels, and newspaper sales resulted. The sheer logistics of mobilizing for war also placed a greater demand on the news media, as people sought information about employment, the services, and volunteering. The news explosion occurred together with codes of voluntary self-censorship adopted by the various media, which wished to avoid being run entirely by the government. Any information that could remotely aid the enemy was weeded out.

Patriotism was in style, and emotions ran high during the early forties. Loved ones were away indefinitely, family life was disrupted, and shortages occurred. Movies and radio offered an escape, fantasy, and the

Before and during the war, the radio was the main source of information. People listened to Roosevelt's "fireside chats" on the state of the nation, and to Ed Murrow reporting on the Blitz in London. The news was censored by the networks themselves so that any information that could remotely aid the enemy was removed.

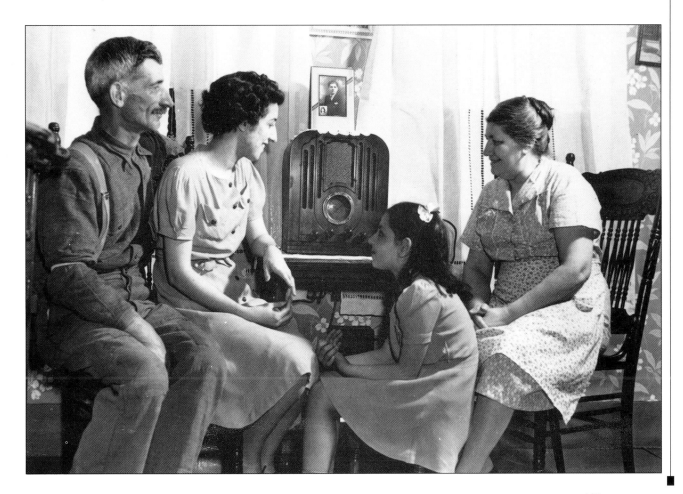

promise of a better future. The media translated Americans' wishful thinking into indelible images. Programming became overly sentimental, saturated with cozy images of the ideal hearth and home.

The war itself was a much-repeated subject in which good and bad were clearly delineated. Characters depicted what Americans saw as their highest virtues: honor, self-reliance, and sacrifice for others. It is no accident that the American media tended to portray moral absolutes: Heroes were heroic, villains were villainous, and there was no ambiguity about it. Uncertainty about right and wrong was not allowed any quarter in America's push for victory.

Toward this end, the government issued guidelines that influenced media content, recognizing right away that radio and movies could be used to keep morale high. Indeed, the government spent a lot of money making films and radio programs to deliver a patriotic message. But propaganda was nothing new to Americans in wartime. World War I had seen the glorification of the doughboy and patriotic songs such as "Over There." But there was something shrill about World War II media, no doubt because the government had such a large stake in much of the propaganda and guided its content to achieve victory. The message got hammered home again and again.

Much of the pounding was done by celebrities hired by the government to sell the war cause. Stars gave concerts to the troops, sold war bonds, and visited wounded soldiers, not to mention acting or singing in hundreds of war-related movies, radio programs, and popular songs. Naturally, it was good publicity for a star to

be seen as a patriot during war. But the stars also gave war an added glamour and excitement that belied the drab uncertainties that most Americans lived with during wartime.

The Radio Lifeline

Between 1925 and 1948, the year of television's first appearance, radio was where tens of millions of Americans turned each day for information and relaxation. Having emerged in 1920 as a viable medium, by 1940 thirty million homes in America possessed radios, or one for every four people. Families tuned into their favorite programs on a daily or weekly basis, much as with television today.

Radio was immediate. It was also highly intimate: Announcers sounded like they were in the room with the listener. Radio first brought Americans the speeches of Hitler and Mussolini in the thirties. And it was on the radio that most Americans learned that the nation was at war on December 8, 1941, when they heard Roosevelt announce the bombing of Pearl Harbor. From this day forward, news became radio's biggest contribution to the war.

Official war messages were delivered over the radio, too — pleas to buy war bonds, announcements about rationing, appeals for scrap drives and volunteers for the USO or Red Cross, interruptions in programming for news flashes, and other items of interest. Radio offered an incessant vocal crusade on behalf of the war effort.

Military-oriented programming also proliferated, increasing empathy for American boys overseas. Programs such as "The Man Behind the Gun," "The Army Hour," and "Stage Door

"I'm standing on a rooftop looking out over London. You may be able to hear the sound of guns off in the distance very faintly, like someone kicking a tub. . . . You'll hear two bursts a little nearer in a moment. There they are! That hard, stony sound."

Edward R. Murrow, reporting on the radio from London during the Battle of Britain

Egbert "Edward" Roscoe Murrow. (1908-1965)

Edward R. Murrow was a broadcasting pioneer, one of the more influential news-casters who helped catapult the profession to national importance during World War II. His memorable wartime contribution was his live broadcasting during the Battle of Britain in 1940. The tall, lean, dark-haired CBS correspondent riveted American radio audiences as he stood night after night on a London rooftop, bringing the drama of the blitz directly into American living rooms. Over Murrow's deep, dramatic voice, Ameri-cans could hear the screaming engines of the Nazi *Luftwaffe* and know that it was hap-pening live as Murrow spoke.

Murrow, remarkably, had virtually no newspaper reporting experience. But he pos-sessed a great deal of intuition, verbal skills, and common sense. To Americans, he was the prototype of the dapper war correspondent; trench-coated, with a cigarette in the corner of his mouth. He repeatedly put his own life on the line to bring the news to Amer-icans. Not only was the BBC building from which he broadcast bombed three times, Mur-row also flew along on Allied combat missions. Accompanying one such bombing mission over Berlin in 1943, he reported, "Berlin . . . was a kind of orchestrated hell, a terrible symphony of light and flame. It isn't a pleasant kind of warfare — the men doing it speak of it as a job."

Born in Greensboro, North Carolina, Murrow was the son of a farmer and sometime railroad engineer who moved the family to the Pacific Northwest when Murrow was a child. At Washington State College, Edward Murrow was an avid debater and actor. Graduating Phi Beta Kappa, Murrow toured Europe for the National Student Federation, during which time he learned skills that served him as a newscaster.

Long interested in journalism, Murrow joined CBS in 1935, in the heyday of radio, and became its European director in 1937. In 1938, his colleague William Shirer called him from Vienna with the news of Hitler's *Anschluss* through Austria. Murrow had the scoop. He then flew to Vienna to witness and report on the arrival of the Nazis firsthand.

During these early days, when America was not yet in the war, Murrow and his colleagues had the difficult job of reporting these har-rowing events while trying to maintain a neutral tone; American isolationism was strong and the journalistic code insisted on objectivi-ty — no easy task in the face of Nazi aggression.

After the war, with his reputation for compassion-ate yet clear-eyed reporting firmly established, Murrow produced the weekly news digest, "Hear It Now," and its television successor, "See It Now," from 1947 to 1960. He also reported from the foxholes of the Korean war in 1950 for CBS.

In the fifties, Murrow's television reporting helped to expose the Communist witch-hunting tactics of Senator Joe McCarthy. In 1961, President Kennedy appointed Murrow director of the U.S. Information Agency, a job that paid him a paltry $21,000, compared to the $300,000 he had earned at CBS. But the work was a matter of principle to Murrow. While director, he applied rigorous journalistic techniques to the agency's information gathering, saying "We cannot make good news out of bad practice." He held this job until illness forced him to resign in 1964.

> *". . . able to leap tall buildings at a single bound! . . . It's a bird! It's a plane! It's Super-man!"*
>
> Popular saying of 1940

Canteen" were all propagandistic war movies. Children's programming, especially, was propagandized, with military heroes as their subject: "Don Winslow of the Navy," "Captain Midnight," and "Terry and the Pirates" were typical.

American radio of the forties was also highly varied. In addition to news and music of every description, programming included fine drama, westerns, soap operas, quiz shows, sports, comedy-variety shows, and detective-crime mysteries — most of these formats a product of radio's growth years in the thirties. Game shows and quiz shows, however, were sharply curtailed during the war, since it was feared that live audiences and players could give secret codes and messages to the enemy over this medium.

War's end brought a period of reevaluation for radio. The Cold War cropped up in new social commentary shows such as "Meet the Press," and "Capitol Cloakroom." Quiz shows and game shows again became big. However, by the end of the decade, many of the same programs that had become popular in the twenties and thirties were still dominating the air waves, and radio seemed unable to offer anything new.

When television arrived in 1948, it quickly supplanted radio. Early television programming was not so different from the familiar formats of radio quiz shows and variety hours; in fact, television was called "sight radio" by many. Early television owed much of its success to the crossover of radio artists such as Milton Berle, Ed Sullivan, and Edward R. Murrow into television. By 1950, television shows such as "The Goldbergs," "Arthur Godfrey's Talent Scouts," and "The Life of Riley" came directly from

radio, complete with the same stars and sponsors. But the novelty of seeing the program eclipsed the humble radio. As the number of transmitters and TV stations increased in the fifties, TV replaced radio with fresh images, new talent, and new shows.

The Magical Movies

The forties were indisputably Hollywood's golden age. Upwards of five hundred films per year were made, and eighty million movie tickets were sold every week during the late thirties and early forties. Enormous movie studios were kept constantly busy producing films to satisfy America's insatiable appetite. Movie studios became factories with departments for each function, from costumes to filming to final editing and cutting.

The studios made huge sums of money, since owning almost all the theaters guaranteed them a marketplace for their films, good, bad, or run-of-the-mill. In 1946, American films had their biggest year to date, grossing 1.7 billion dollars. Movies were so important during the early forties that the Office of War Information decreed the business an essential industry and created the Bureau of Motion Pictures, whose job it was to make sure only positive war images were represented in movies.

Indeed, the movies were a particularly powerful means of stirring patriotism. Of the 1,313 features made between 1942 and 1944, 374 concerned some aspect of war, and a good many more referred to it. Famous war films included *Casablanca, Mrs. Miniver, Lifeboat, Notorious,* and *The Best Years of Our Lives,* which offered a realistic portrait of several

The Shepherd of the Hills, *starring John Wayne, Betty Field, and Harry Carey, was typical of films of its time.*

soldiers' postwar readjustment to home life. Battle-oriented films were also made in great numbers: *Wake Island*, *The Battle of Midway*, *Watch on the Rhine*, *Guadalcanal Diary*, and *Destination Tokyo* offered calculated glimpses into the lives of America's soldiers. Inevitably, these films painted all Nazis and Japanese characters as one-dimensionally evil, while Americans with intelligence and compassion triumphed in the end. In their simplistic presentations of both sides, these war films were meant to reassure

Walt Disney. (1901-1966)

Walter Elias Disney was the ultimate self-made man. Born in Chicago in 1901 to a stern, frugal father and a cool, detached mother, Disney's upbringing as the fourth of five children was harsh and lonely. As a child, Walt was made to work long hours and give his wages to his debt plagued father. The family moved all over the Midwest in search of a better living.

The elder Disney beat his children, and they all eventually ran away from home, including Walt at age seventeen. However, Walt's father had encouraged Walt in his art lessons, and drawing became the boy's passion. Disney bought his first camera from savings from odd jobs, and his goal from then on was to be a commercial cartoonist. Financial hardship had given him the burning desire to be a successful entrepreneur; his willingness to take risks and his obsession for detail gave him further drive.

Throughout the twenties and thirties, Disney struggled to make a living at animation, making cartoon shorts on a shoestring budget for local theaters. He developed a few standard characters for cartoon series, the only way a cartoonist could hope to make a living in those days. In 1928, Disney invented Mickey Mouse, who starred in the first sound cartoon, *Steamboat Willie*. From there, he went on to produce the characters of Pluto, Donald Duck, and Goofy, and the cartoon, *Silly Symphonies*. For five years, Disney worked on his first major feature-length cartoon. It paid off; *Snow White*, appearing in 1937, was an instant hit. Its realistic movement, special effects, and great detail were technological marvels.

The forties were Disney's most fruitful years of classic feature animation. *Fantasia* and *Pinocchio* appeared in 1940, *Dumbo* in 1941, *Bambi* in 1942, *The Three Caballeros* in 1945, and *Cinderella* in 1950.

Walt repressed his unhappy childhood, and his relationships with people were superficial. He was mistrustful and aloof, and his movies reflected this; they glossed over traumatic events, dwelling on the sentimental, pleasant, and humorous. Fathers were authoritarian or oblivious, mothers absent or minor characters at best. Disney packaged easily digestible, boy-meets-girl stories in which emotional complexities were nonexistent, as were intricate plots and characters. Good always triumphed over evil. "There's enough ugliness and cynicism in the world without me adding to it," Disney once said.

Disney, an obsessive perfectionist, supervised every detail of his movies. His penchant for self-promotion frustrated his overworked and underpaid staff, who got little public credit for their work, which led to a strike in 1941. His demand for greater and greater realism taxed his artistic staff to the point where the studio set up its own art school to train artists in "action analysis" and built its own zoo to observe animal movement firsthand. Film crews were hired to capture animals in their natural habitats, which animators could then translate into realistic drawings. This led, in the forties, to the birth of the Disney nature films. It was also during the forties that Disney began to market toys and other items featuring Disney characters, and they became his main moneymaker. These helped support his costly studio overhead.

But there was another side to the Disney studio — less well known yet prolific during the war years. Disney was contracted by the government to produce propaganda and instructional films in quantities unprecedented in film history. Disney's characters, especially Donald Duck, were enlisted in the fight against Nazi domination. Disney created scores of series and features, including *Donald Gets Drafted* (1942), *Out of the Frying Pan into the Firing Line* (1942), *The Spirit of '43* (1943), *Der Fuehrer's Face,* and many, many others. In all, 94 percent of the film footage Disney studios produced during the war was for the government.

As the forties ended, Disney's interest in television programs, live-action films, and Disneyland began, causing a lull in classic feature animation. But he had made his mark, both technologically and culturally, which is still indelible today.

folks on the home front and keep morale up. They also confirmed the American public's feelings that they were justified in fighting a good war for all the right reasons.

Great and most glamorous stars reigned during the forties: tough guys, such as Humphrey Bogart and Gary Cooper; silky-smooth glamour actress — Katharine Hepburn — made some of her most memorable movies in this era, too.

A gutsy new generation of great actors was beginning to appear: Marlon Brando and Montgomery Clift epitomized the tormented sensitive modern man, while Marilyn Monroe and Elizabeth Taylor were the ulti-

queens of icy perfection, such as Joan Crawford, Bette Davis, Marlene Dietrich, and Carole Lombard; sexy pinup girls, such as Betty Grable and Rita Hayworth; the girl-next-door types, like Ginger Rogers and Judy Garland. Then there were the romantic leading men who set the standard for all who followed: Cary Grant, Jimmy Stewart, and Clark Gable. The most free-spirited and unconventional, yet immensely talented,

mate sex-kitten bombshells. An older generation of actors were doing their late films; Tallulah Bankhead, Ethel Barrymore, Charlie Chaplin, W. C. Fields, Greta Garbo, and Mae West all had done their groundbreaking work in the twenties and thirties.

Great directors working in Hollywood during this period included Frank Capra, Alfred Hitchcock, and John Huston. Their artistic visions

Citizen Kane marked the Hollywood debut of Orson Welles as starring actor, director, and producer. A dark and thinly disguised portrait of the press tycoon William Randolph Hearst, it became renowned for its editing technique and powerful use of sound.

Humphrey Bogart. (1899-1957)

Humphrey DeForest Bogart epitomized the tough guy with the tender heart in Hollywood movies of the forties. He was one of the decade's biggest box office stars, indeed, one of the biggest of all time. Bogart appeared in such famous films as *The Maltese Falcon* (1941), *To Have and Have Not* (1945), *The Big Sleep* (1946), *Key Largo* (1948), and *The African Queen* (1951), for which he won the Academy Award for best actor.

Bogart's appeal lay in the hint of human frailty that he let show behind his cynical exterior. Though he later grew into a brilliant, versatile actor, Bogart first made a name for himself portraying dozens of gangsters, villains, and hoods, with a sneering smile and deadpan delivery. Indeed, throughout the thirties, he was typecast as Hollywood's ultimate tough guy. Bogart's famous stiff upper lip was his trademark, ironically so, since it was the result of a large splinter piercing the lip and permanently deadening the nerve.

Humphrey Bogart (right) in a scene from the 1942 film, Casablanca.

The fame that came to the adult Bogart would never have been imagined by the boy who was the son of a well-to-do New York City surgeon. Bogart attended elite private schools and joined the navy in World War I. But after the war, he became a vagabond for a couple of years, making his acting debut as an adolescent in a 1920 road show titled *The Ruined Lady*. Throughout the decade, he played many similar parts: hardly a glorious beginning.

In 1935, however, Bogart landed the role of Duke Mantee, a heartless gangster, in the Broadway production of *The Petrified Forest*. A year later, he reprised the role in the movie of the same name and shot to stardom. In this role, Bogart portrayed the complexities and moral decay of the criminal personality; his violence had motivations, horrible though they might be. This was more than a cookie cutter approach to a stereotypical character. From then on, Bogart concentrated on transforming himself into a serious actor with a command over his screen persona.

With *The Petrified Forest* and *The Maltese Falcon,* Bogart broke out of his B-movie gangster roles and became a major leading man. He brought to his mature movies of the forties the same hard-boiled, sarcastic exterior of his gangster pictures, but he expressed a wider array of emotions beneath the tough shell — the obsessive greed of Fred C. Dobbs in *The Treasure of the Sierra Madre* (1948), the dispassionate intelligence of private eye Sam Spade in *The Maltese Falcon,* the repressed bitterness of cabaret owner Rick in *Casablanca* (1942), or the quietly neurotic Captain Queeg in *The Caine Mutiny* (1954).

Bogart's personal life was also quietly tumultuous. Avoiding the allure of Hollywood glamour, he chose to live the life of a typical family man. But he married four times, the last time to Lauren Bacall in 1945, an actress much younger than he but with a similar cool, dispassionate screen presence. Together, "Bogie" and "Baby," as they were known in Hollywood, made five movies of such obvious personal chemistry that they caused a sensation in the media, the first being *The Big Sleep* in 1946.

Bogart's late fifties pictures, including *The African Queen* and *The Caine Mutiny,* were hailed as some of his best work. But Bogart's health began to fail. He was plagued with a hacking cough, and died of throat cancer in 1957.

were both realistic and romantic, and their dramas were sweeping, suspenseful, and sentimental, bordering on melodramatic. Cinema was profoundly pro-American. Indeed, many of these famous directors were hired by the government to make war documentaries, such as Frank Capra's *Why We Fight* series and Walt Disney's *Victory Through Air Power*. Ultimately, most Hollywood films of the forties showed a fairly narrow and predictable set of morals and characters.

The one remarkable exception to the generally formulaic view of the world was the movie *Citizen Kane* (1941), made by actor-director Orson Welles. It was his first, and ultimately most important, film (made when he was only twenty-six) and probably one of the most important masterpieces in American film history.

Welles's exploration of an egomaniacal man's obsession with wealth, power, and the frustrated search for happiness was done in a way no studio had ever made a movie before. Seeing to every detail of its making, Welles used new techniques, incorporating stage lighting methods, radio sound methods, montage, new fast film, and a sixty-year time span for the story. The film was moody and dark; it was a view of the world that was also dark and negative. The complexity and somberness of the film at first puzzled and discomfited American audiences, as Welles indeed had intended. Unusual for the time, the film offered no easy answers, no pat solutions, no happy ending. *Citizen Kane* brought new moviemaking methods into the mainstream, most notably into the film noir genre.

Film noir was a type of motion picture that was pessimistic, fatalistic, or cynical in mood and content, often dealing with the subjects of inner city crime and corruption. It was Hollywood's concession to the dark side of life. In these films, themes of alienation and anxiety were played out by morally questionable heroes and heroines. Film noir characters weren't glamorous or even intentionally likeable. Film noir men were tough, ordinary guys beset by the problems an unforgiving world threw at them. The leading man was the antihero, powerless against the system, trying his best to survive and not always succeeding. Film noir women were cold, shrewd, and willing to do whatever was necessary to get what they wanted. Their sexuality was portrayed as dangerous and overpowering, as in *Double Indemnity* (1944), with Barbara Stanwyck, who convinces a bewitched Fred McMurray to kill her husband for her.

Film noir, despite its formulaic approach to characterization and plot, gave film a fresh, new look. Odd camera angles, clipped dialogue, multiple narrators, flashbacks, studies in black and white photography — all were tools of the film noir trade, and they all served to restyle American cinematography.

As the war ended and communism became the enemy, the moral absolutes so prevalent in war films took an even more strident tone in such propagandistic films as *I Married a Communist, The Iron Curtain, The Red Menace,* and *The Red Danube.* Evil Nazis and Japs were replaced with sinister Communists as the villains.

After the war, the American courts demanded that Hollywood studios sell their theaters to counter the accusation that they held a monopoly. Instantly, films no longer had an automatic outlet. Major studios began to fail or cut back. Production costs

The influence of Hollywood's most popular movie stars was not lost on advertisers. Here, the cast of The Paradine Case *(1948) endorses Chesterfield cigarettes.*

suddenly skyrocketed. With television's advent in 1948, box office sales began to slump, and the boom years of Hollywood were over.

Women Real or Ideal

The confusion of sex roles — the idea that males and females are, by nature, limited to certain behaviors because of their sex — caused by the increased number of women working — led the media to idealize traditional women's roles. In the media, the ideal woman made her face, figure, and clothes attractive to please a man, even though she was doing her war duty by working. Women were admonished to always be attentive to a man's needs. Here again, the stars helped bring the message across. Joan Crawford and Claudette Colbert, two of Hollywood's most glamorous stars, advised women to tend to their domestic duties with joy and to try to be charming for their men. The message was that women, married or not, should try to be soft and feminine in order to give soldiers, who were making great sacrifices for freedom, something to live for.

Strong women were portrayed in movies such as *Here Come the Waves, So Proudly We Hail, Swing Shift Maisie, Government Girl,* and *Tender Comrade,* but their glamour never left them. But the woman who gave up her job or career for marriage, particularly to a soldier, was portrayed the most favorably of all.

Emerging alongside Rosie the Riveter was her opposite number, the pinup girl. The most famous of these were Marilyn Monroe, Betty Grable, Rita Hayworth, and Lana Turner, all gifted talents in their own right, yet they were idealized by soldiers as fleshy goddesses whose images were pinned up in Allied army barracks the world over. The pinup girl inspired the fighting man. Her sexuality was safe, innocent, all-American, something to fight and die for. After the war, this definition of sexuality gave way to images of women as destructive, dangerous forces if they succeeded in getting their way with men. In either case, the message to both women and men was that women should subordinate their desires to those of men.

African-Americans in the Media

African-Americans had rarely been given roles, either in Hollywood or on radio. When they were, the parts were stereotypically inferior ones as maids, servants, or loafers. With the war, this began to change. Black actors such as Paul Robeson and Lena Horne began to argue for greater dignity in black movie and radio roles. Some black actors even filled in on traditionally white roles.

White actors such as Humphrey Bogart, Charles Laughton, and Edward G. Robinson joined with black actors in the Emergency Committee of the Entertainment Industry and other organizations to work for better treatment of blacks in entertainment industries. These protests

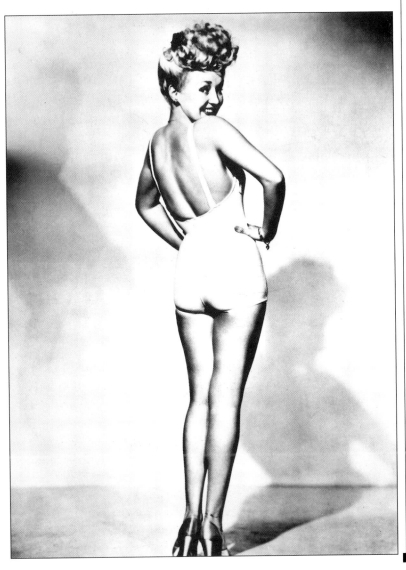

Betty Grable became the pinup queen of GIs around the world. Though talented in their own right, Grable, and other stars like her, were turned into mere sex goddesses, whose sole purpose was to inspire the fighting men.

"To all newspapers and radio stations — all those who reach the eyes and ears of the American people — I say this: You have a most grave responsibility to the nation, now and for the duration of this war. If you feel that your government is not disclosing enough of the truth, you have every right to say so. But — in the absence of all the facts as revealed by official sources — you have no right in the ethics of patriotism to deal out unconfirmed reports in such a way as to make people believe they are the gospel truth."

President Roosevelt in his fireside chat two days after the Pearl Harbor bombing

had some effect. African-Americans began to appear in a wider array of roles: Dooley Wilson as the piano player in *Casablanca* (1942); Canada Lee in *Lifeboat,* Hitchcock's anti-Nazi film of 1944; Kenneth Spencer, playing a soldier in *Bataan* (1943); and Hattie McDaniel in *In This Our Life* (1942), about a law student victimized by prejudice. Other prominent African-American actors of the era included names such as Ethel Waters, Ernest Anderson, Rex Ingrams, and Cab Calloway.

By the end of the decade, however, the backlash at women also caught African-Americans. So-called negro-problem movies were made, four of them released in 1949 alone, including *Lost Boundaries, Intruder in the Dust,* and *Home of the Brave.* In these films, blacks who challenged white power met predictably tragic ends. In all films in which blacks were portrayed in the forties, however, blacks were largely victims, saved by the actions of whites.

This stereotypical view of African-Americans did not prevent propaganda from being aimed at them, too, however. The War Department made the film *The Negro Soldier* in 1944 (the navy produced *The Negro Sailor* the following year). Intended to prove to whites that blacks cared about the war cause and to blacks that war service was an essential patriotic duty, it simply ignored the question of racial segregation in the armed forces. In fact, the 1946 propaganda film *Teamwork* carefully cut footage to make it appear that blacks and whites worked side by side in the armed forces. This was, of course, misleading, but it curiously gave impetus to African-Americans' arguments in favor of an integrated army in 1948. Another form of propaganda was the "All-American News," the only newsreel made especially for black audiences, seen by blacks all over America, and proclaiming black support for the war.

Journalism at the Front

The public's greater attention on the news resulted in an expansion of journalism in radio, print, and photography. The war gave journalists vast amounts of fresh material and opportunities to collect exciting news firsthand. Many an adventurous reporter, male and female, followed the armies to get the most sensational stories. Indeed, some news reporters became journalistic heroes in their own right, such as the legendary Ernie Pyle, Edward R. Murrow, and Margaret Bourke-White, continuing America's long-standing tradition of ace reporting. Radio news columnists proliferated: H. V. Kaltenborn, William L. Shirer, Elmer Davis, Boake Carter, and Lowell Thomas delivered news and views to their listeners in ringing tones.

The *Stars and Stripes* appeared in 1942, a daily paper especially for U.S. troops in Europe, written by a ragtag staff of enlisted men. The paper ran news from the front and published morale-lifting stories and popular comic strips such as "Terry and the Pirates." For two cents, a soldier could buy the paper anywhere the U.S. Army was stationed. For a while, the *Stars and Stripes* brought the American free press right into the heart of Europe.

Newsreels were another popular form of news programming. These films brought visual images of the war

Margaret Bourke-White. (1904-1971)

Margaret Bourke-White was a daredevil photographer and war correspondent. She constantly put herself in dangerous, life-threatening situations during the war to get unique photos.

Maggie, as she was called, had never been timid. She was the adored only child of an inventor father, whose technical interests in light (he contributed to color film's development) influenced her, and she became keenly interested in different camera techniques and film developing.

Unpopular at school, Maggie found solace in her pet snakes and alligators, and in her photography. During her years at Cornell University (graduating in 1927), she sold her photos of the campus to help pay for her tuition. Her marriage at age nineteen to Everett Chapman, a welder (a craft Maggie was interested in), lasted less than two years. Upon divorcing Chapman, she retook her maiden name, hyphenating her middle name, Bourke, with White to give it more distinction.

As a staff photographer for *Fortune* magazine from 1929 to 1933, Maggie indulged her interest in factories, which were beautiful to her; she would climb factory roofs to get just the right shots. She also became one of the few western photographers to take pictures in postrevolutionary Russia and the first ever to photograph Russian industry. Then, from 1936 to 1969, she became a staff photographer for *Life* magazine, her photographs bringing her great fame.

During the thirties, Bourke-White and novelist Erskine Caldwell collaborated on *You Have Seen Their Faces?,* a book about poverty in the South. They married in 1939 (divorcing in 1942), producing the collaborative books, *North of the Danube,* about the Sudetenland crisis, and *Say! Is This the USA?* (1941). In addition to her *Life* assignments, Bourke-White also published *Shooting the Russian War* (1942), for which she and Caldwell had hidden in Moscow to observe and photograph the invasion of three million Axis troops; she was the only foreign photographer allowed in the Soviet Union at that time.

After Pearl Harbor, Bourke-White became the first accredited woman war correspondent in U.S. history and also served as the army's model for the war correspondents' uniform for women; more were to follow her. She was also the first woman allowed on a bombing mission (January 1943) and one of the first reporters assigned to cover the North African campaign in 1943. "I learned to appreciate a nice deep muddy ditch which I could roll into during a shelling," she wrote of her war experience.

Bourke-White fulfilled many war assignments, working in tandem for the War Department and *Life* magazine. Her commitment to getting the right photograph came before anything or anyone else, even her own personal safety. She and all her bulky equipment were frequent witnesses on Allied bombing raids. Arriving with Patton's army at Buchenwald concentration camp, Bourke-White took disturbing pictures of the horror before her. These dramatic pictures rallied Americans in support of the war effort, while her more gruesome pictures were censored.

After the war, Bourke-White photographed the civil war in India and the Hindu leader, Mohandas Ghandhi, only hours before his assassination in 1948. She took the last photograph of Ghandhi on his funeral pyre, despite cameras having been forbidden; she had to get a picture of the great martyr going up in flames. Her book, *Halfway to Freedom: A Study of the New India,* was published in 1949. Bourke-White's war correspondence career ended in the fifties with the onset of Parkinson's disease, though she continued to take photographs and write books.

"Jolting" Joe DiMaggio played for the New York Yankees for thirteen years (serving in the army from 1943-1945) and was consistently the team's most outstanding player. Though plagued by injuries throughout his career, he was on the all-star batting team every year and, except for 1946 and 1951, batted over .300 each season.

directly from battlefield to movie house, though they were not as immediate as radio news.

Sports

News was not the only item of general interest. Baseball captured a wide media audience in the forties. Not only was it America's favorite game, but remarkable changes were occurring in the sport. Jackie Robinson, joining the Brooklyn Dodgers in 1947, became the first African-American major league player; Joe DiMaggio hit ninety-six times in

fifty-one consecutive games; and women got their own professional baseball league in the Midwest, lasting from 1943 to 1954. In 1943, spring training was held in the North for the first time because of the war, and by 1944, many retired baseball players returned to the field because so many younger players had been drafted. The war had even altered America's favorite pastime — but only temporarily.

By 1946, many stars had returned from the war, and in 1948, U.S. athletes were proudly bringing home gold medals from the London Olympics.

Jack "Jackie" Roosevelt Robinson. (1919-1972)

Jackie Robinson made baseball history in 1947 by becoming the first African-American to sign with the major leagues, shattering a color barrier in place since 1876. Robinson's mother, Mallie McGriff Robinson, was the daughter of an emancipated slave and a major force in her son's life. Robinson also idolized his older brother, Mack (who later ran with Jesse Owens in the Berlin Olympics of 1936), who taught Jackie how to run and play baseball.

In high school, Jackie proved himself a star in football, track, and baseball. He went to Pasadena Junior College, and from there to the University of California in Los Angeles on a full athletic scholarship. There he played four sports: football (becoming known as one of the "Touchdown Twins"), baseball, basketball, and track. In 1938, he held the national record for punt returns in football.

Jackie left college only weeks before graduation to work as a coach for the National Youth Administration. He desperately needed the money. When war came, Jackie enlisted, and with the help of heavyweight boxing champion, Joe Louis, Robinson entered the Officers Candidate School, which normally excluded African-Americans, graduating as a second lieutenant.

Receiving a medical discharge from the army, Robinson signed with the Kansas City Monarchs, part of the Negro American League, in April 1945. Robinson was aggravated by the grueling minor league schedule and less than adequate facilities. He was frustrated, too, knowing that black ballplayers — no matter how well they played — would never make it to the major leagues.

Robinson's big breakthrough came in 1945, when the Brooklyn Dodgers' president, Branch Rickey, signed him to play with the Montreal Royals, the Brooklyn farm team, thus becoming the first African-American player in organized baseball. Rickey had long been an advocate of having black players in the major leagues. He warned Robinson that his would be no easy ride in the all-white league. As a Royal, Robinson coped with much resentment and anger at his presence, especially from his team manager, Clay Hopper. Nevertheless, in his first season, Robinson played in one hundred games, got 133 hits, stole thirty-three bases, and scored one hundred runs, finishing the season with a .349 average, a performance that helped the Royals to win the league championship that year.

Branch Rickey thought it was time for Robinson to play in the major league, and he announced Robinson's signing with the Dodgers in April 1947. Many of Robinson's teammates were blatantly racist, insisting they be traded rather than play on the same team with a black man. The racism depressed Robinson, and he was warned by his doctor to avoid having a nervous breakdown. Despite these difficulties, Robinson's performance earned him Rookie of the Year honors in 1947, and the Dodgers won the league pennant.

Robinson was with the Dodgers for ten years; in six of those years, they won the National League pennant and went on to win the World Series. He was known for his excellent hitting ability, aggressive play, and base-stealing abilities. In 1949, his best year, Robinson led the league in batting (.342) and in stolen bases (thirty-seven); and for this he was voted Most Valuable Player. That year, he was voted to the All-Star team for the first time.

In 1956, Robinson retired from baseball to become vice president of personnel at Chock Full O' Nuts. He also became active in the NAACP and worked all his life for national political campaigns and on behalf of civil rights issues. He also wrote a sports column for the *New York Post*. In 1962, he was elected to the Baseball Hall of Fame.

CHAPTER 9
The Forties, America's Pivotal Decade

The advertisement slogan for Mercury automobiles in 1947 summed up the consumer confidence of postwar America. "More of everything you want with Mercury."

America's role in World War II forever changed the country and Americans' perceptions of themselves from Depression-era isolationists to key players in world affairs. The war was the main event in a highly eventful decade. It acted as the catalyst for change on so many levels —

economic, social, political, military — that viewed as a whole, the forties were years of profound upheaval. The shock waves from these explosive times are still being felt.

The five broadest trends of the decade with the greatest importance for history were that: (1) America became the dominant world power in the aftermath of the war; (2) Americans experienced large-scale postwar abundance that found its political reflection in strong anticommunist sentiments; (3) atomic weapons and the Cold War reinvented war, international relations, and America's place in them, as well as Americans' attitudes towards science and military strength; (4) racism, sexism, and antisemitism became all-pervasive during the forties, and the atmosphere of the times prevented large gains in equality; and (5) a huge, decade-long migration of African-Americans from South to North was a major factor in the later civil rights movement.

America, New World Power

The most obvious change was in America's sudden reversal of attitude toward the rest of the world: Two decades of isolationism gave way to popular support for fighting a world war on two fronts. From this great conflict, to whose victory America

had contributed mightily, the nation emerged the richest, most heavily armed, best equipped, best trained, and consequently most powerful nation on earth. America had endured shortages and deprivations during the war, and it had lost hundreds of thousands in battle, but these setbacks were nothing in comparison to the devastation wrought on European countries, the Soviet Union, China, and Japan. With these countries in a terribly weakened state, America's dominance was even more clear.

From this newly found power, America gained a new sense of superiority over other nations. This did not just include military superiority, though with the atomic bomb, military superiority was the key new element in America's dominance on the world stage. America took the opportunity to lord its military and economic strength over other nations, offering aid to those countries it wished to support politically, and threatening others with whom it disagreed (such as the Soviet Union), with dire consequences. The billions of dollars funded by the Marshall Plan were only the beginning of the sort of leverage the powerful new United States was willing to wield to influence foreign countries. The Truman Doctrine, as Godfrey Hodgson writes, "contained the seeds of a habit of intervention" by the U.S. in the affairs of more than a hundred foreign countries over a period of forty years.

Anticommunism and Abundance

The superiority felt in the military-industrial arena carried over into the social sphere as well. Throughout the war, Americans believed that by pitching in together, they could accomplish victory, and they had. After the war, the gung-ho spirit of sacrifice for the greater good of the country evolved into a fiercely pro-American attitude. Stepped-up anticommunist campaigns were the most outward sign of this new stance.

Another sign of American superiority was in its new purchasing power. The nation's industries quickly converted to peacetime production to supply pent-up demand. Millions of women who so recently were employed in war factories were now returning to full-time homemaking, having more babies than any generation of American women in history, and buying more consumer goods than ever before. A new emphasis on domestic life, the so-called nuclear family, emerged. This model, in which a mother stayed at home to raise children and tend exclusively to domestic affairs, while a father worked exclusively outside the home, became not just a popular trend but a pattern to which many young people felt pressured to conform. Material prosperity and personal conformity became equated with being pro-American. As Elaine Tyler May wrote, "Cold War ideology and the domestic revival [are] two sides of the same coin: postwar Americans' intense need to feel liberated from the past and secure in the future."

Atomic Fears

But security was an elusive goal as the Cold War escalated and the atomic bombs grew more numerous, more deadly, and more widespread.

"These postwar babies feel that they will not live out their lifetime to expectation. I have one boy who's . . . not making any provisions, even at thirty-four. . . . He's just one of the thousands of young people who grew up ducking under their desks in atomic-bomb drills at school. Why would they think there's a future? All their lives they've heard about the bomb being dropped. That's a sad way to live."

Marnie Seymour in
The Good War
by Studs Terkel

A Levittown shopping center in 1949. In the postwar years, the suburbs were the place to be, especially if you were young, white, married, and had, or wanted to have, children. Mothers were expected to stay home, run the house, take care of the children, and have their husband's meal ready on the table when he returned from work. But this cozy picture of middle-class life belied the frustration soon to be felt by American women.

One of Americans' greatest worries was whether, with its ability to destroy entire cities with one explosion, the future of the whole world could ever really be secure.

The nuclear threat was another of the great changes brought about by the war. It had not existed before the war, and afterward, Americans would never imagine war or peace in quite the same way as they had prior to the atomic bomb. In the aftermath of Hiroshima and Nagasaki, Americans felt invincible on the one hand, but lost a lot of their idealism on the other. The uncertainties created by the

nuclear age produced new trends in art, social science, science, diplomacy, and popular culture. No facet of society was untouched. This all-pervasive change unsettled Americans, and while some might characterize postwar America as flaunting its dominance, its power was also something of a psychological burden.

Technology was also growing more pervasive in the national consciousness. Clearly, the bomb had made its inventors powerful, but the thing itself was more powerful than the men who created it. Another technological milestone — television

— played a new role in shaping the attitudes, thoughts, dreams, desires, and shared knowledge of Americans. Making its debut in eight hundred thousand homes in 1948, television reached into more than eight million living rooms by the decade's end, and would continue to grow by millions each year.

Racism, Sexism, and Antisemitism Run Rampant

Despite the let's-all-pull-together attitude of the wartime forties, the decade was highly divided on the matters of race, sex, and ethnicity. Indeed, if you did not conform to the prevailing model, that is, if you were not a Protestant male, and especially if you were not white, you could expect discrimination, both blatant and subtle, to affect your everyday life. You could also expect to find almost no remedies in the courts for this discrimination should you require redress, since civil rights movements were still in their infancy.

It is characteristic of this paradoxical decade that where the greatest injustices existed — in jobs, housing, and wages — there were also examples of the greatest attempts to conform to the prevailing attitudes rather than stand up and fight for equality. For example, few women publicly questioned the fairness of being ordered to leave their factory jobs when the war ended so that returning men could take their places, while many blacks volunteered for the armed services despite open segregation. The forties were a time of great pressure to conform.

The Northern Migration

Another social upheaval caused directly by the war was the great migration of rural southern blacks to northern cities, looking for work in war factories. This migration was four times the rate of black southern-to-northern migration of the thirties. The rapid influx of millions of African-Americans into the largest northern cities, just as many white Americans were starting to move out of the cities for the suburbs, is one of the most significant changes of the forties.

Thus, the African-American community began, in a significant way, to move from its unskilled base in rural, small towns, to making up a very large proportion of major northern urban populations. With African-Americans no longer limited to one region of the country, the South, their rights to have access to justice, education, work, and the rest, could not be ignored. The civil rights movement was no longer seen as a small, regional problem, but rather a fundamental question for the whole of America.

Conclusion

Thus it was, while the power that sprang from America's involvement in World War II seemed unquenchable during the forties, it was not a particularly optimistic time in American history. The doubts and fears caused by the war itself, and the social upheavals that came with it, combined with the nuclear bomb and the resulting Cold War, cast a defining chill on the next five decades of America's history.

KEY DATES

1940

May — Germany takes Netherlands and Belgium; 350,000 Allied troops are evacuated from Dunkirk.

June — Norway surrenders to the Nazis; Italy enters the war; the USSR invades Lithuania, Latvia, and Estonia; Paris surrenders to the Germans.

July - September — The Battle of Britain. Bombs from the German *Luftwaffe* rain down on London.

August 27 — The first color television broadcast, in New York City.

September 27 — Japan, Italy, and Germany sign the Axis pact.

November 5 — Franklin Delano Roosevelt is elected to a third term.

1941

Congress repeals the Neutrality Act.

March 22 — Germany invades the USSR; the USSR becomes a U.S. ally.

December 7 — Japanese attack Pearl Harbor.

December 8 — The United States declares war on Japan.

December 11 — Germany and Italy declare war on the U.S.

1942

January — Japan takes the Philippines; the first reports of atrocities against Jews reach the United States; over one hundred thousand Japanese-Americans are deported to internment camps; the Battle of Java Sea takes place.

March — Allied bombing of Germany begins; the Japanese forcibly marched American male POWs down the Bataan Peninsua in the

Philippines, bayonetting or beheading those who fell from exhaustion; first American bombing raids on Tokyo; Roosevelt imposes price controls.

May 4-8 — The Battle of the Coral Sea.

May 15 — Car production stops. Sugar and tire rationing begin.

June 3-6 — The Battle of Midway, the first major Japanese defeat. American planes sink four Japanese aircraft carriers and destroy almost three hundred planes.

June 13 — Eight German spies are caught on the East Coast.

August 7 — Ten thousand marines land on Guadalcanal to begin a six-month battle in steamy jungle conditions against the Japanese, who had been ordered to fight to the death.

November 7-8 — Allies land in North Africa to fight against General Rommel and his tank divisions.

1943

Supreme Court rules saluting the flag optional in school.

Streptomycin is discovered; sulfa drugs are used to treat venereal disease; DDT is introduced to U.S. agriculture.

January 14-24 — The Allies plan invasion of Europe at the Casablanca Conference.

February — The Allies defeat Rommel in Africa.

February 7 — Shoe rationing begins.

April 1 — Meat, fats, and cheese rationing begins.

April 29 — "Rosie the Riveter" first graces the cover of the *Saturday Evening Post*.

July 10 — The Allies land on Sicily.

September 3 — Italy signs secret armistice with the Allies.

1944

The Supreme Court rules that race is not a bar to voting.

January 22 — The Allies land at Anzio to begin battling their way to Rome.

January 31 — The U.S. invades the Marshall Islands.

February 20 — Round-the-clock air raids on Berlin commence.

May 3 — Meat rationing ends.

June 4 — The Allies take Rome.

June 6 — D-Day, the Allied invasion of Europe begins.

June 15 — U.S. offensives on Saipan, Guam, and Tinian.

June 22 — The GI Bill of Rights is passed.

August — General George Patton reaches the Seine. The Allies land in southern France.

August 14 — Manufacture of large domestic products resumes.

August 25 — Paris is liberated.

September — Brussels is liberated by British forces; the First Army crosses the German border.

October 9 — The United Nations is established.

October 20 — General MacArthur returns to the Philippines.

November 7 — FDR is reelected to a fourth term.

December 16 — The Battle of the Bulge.

1945

January — Yalta conference is held. U.S. army reaches the Rhine.

April 10 — FDR dies.

April 12 — Harry S Truman becomes president.

April 25 — The U.S. Army meets the Russian Army at the Elbe River.

April 30 — Hitler commits suicide.

May — Buchenwald concentration camp is liberated by U.S. troops; Germany surrenders; Soviet troops reach Berlin.

July 16 — An atom bomb is tested at Alamogordo, New Mexico.

July-August 2 — Potsdam conference is held.

August — Atomic bombing of Hiroshima, and Nagasaki, Japan.

August 13 — Japan surrenders.

1946

Blacks vote for first time in the Mississippi Democratic primary.

March 5 — Churchill gives his "Iron Curtain" speech.

July 16 — Atom bomb tests take place on the Bikini Atoll.

1947

Congress forms the CIA.

Truman announces the Marshall Plan to rebuild Europe.

The HUAC investigation indicts the Hollywood Ten.

1948

Supreme Court rules religious schools cannot receive state money.

June — Truman orders the Berlin Airlift, which would eventually deliver two million tons of supplies to the besieged inhabitants of the city.

July — Truman orders the desegregation of the army.

November — Truman surprisingly wins reelection.

1949

The baby boom peaks at 3.58 million live births.

Levittown suburb is built, on Long Island, New York.

April 4 — NATO (North Atlantic Treaty Organization) is created.

August — The Soviet Union tests its own atom bomb.

FOR FURTHER RESEARCH

Boyer, Paul. *By the Bomb's Early Light: American Thought and Culture at the Dawn of the Atomic Age*. New York: Pantheon, 1985.

Bragg, Janet Harmon. *Soaring Above Setbacks: The Autobiography of Janet Harmon Bragg, African American Aviator*. Washington, D.C.: Smithsonian Institution Press, 1996.

Brandt, Nat. *Harlem at War: The Black Experience in World War II*. Syracuse, NY: Syracuse University Press, 1996.

Cohen, Daniel. *The Manhattan Project: A History*. Twenty First Century Books, 1999.

Colman, Penny. *Rosie the Riveter: Women Working on the Home Front in World War II*. New York: Crown, 1998.

Epstein, Dan. *The Early Years to 1949: 20th Century Pop Culture*. Broomall, PA: Chelsea House, 2000.

Galt, Margot Fortunato. *Up to the Plate: The All American Girls Baseball League (Sports Legacy)*. Minneapolis: Lerner, 1995.

Garner, Eleanor Ramrath. *Eleanor's Story: An American Girl in Hitler's Germany*. Atlanta, GA: Peachtree Books, 1999.

Hakim, Joy. *War, Peace, and All That Jazz: 1918-1945*. New York: Oxford University Press, 1999.

Harding, Vincent. *We Changed the World: African Americans, 1945-1970*. New York: Oxford University Press, 1997.

Katz, William Loren. *World War II to the New Frontier, 1940-1963 (History of Multicultural America)*. Austin, TX: Steck Vaughn, 1996.

Nathan, Amy and Eileen Collins. *Yankee Doodle Gal: Women Pilots of World War II*. New York: National Geographic, 2001.

Putney, Martha S. *When the Nation Was in Need: Blacks in the Women's Army Corps during World War II*. Metuchen, NJ: Scarecrow Press, 1992.

Sinnott, Susan. *Our Burden of Shame: The Japanese-American Internment During World War II (First Books)*. New York: Franklin Watts, 1996.

Terkel, Studs. *The Good War: An Oral History of the Second World War*. New York: Ballentine, 1984.

Uschan, Michael V. *The 1940s (Cultural History of the United States Through the Decades)*. San Diego, CA: Lucent, 1999.

Movies

Philadelphia Story, Warner Bros, 1940.

Fantasia, Walt Disney Pictures, 1940.

Citizen Kane, Mercury/RKO, 1941.

Casablanca, Warner Bros, 1943.

It's A Wonderful Life, RKO/Liberty Films, 1946.

Contemporary Music

In the Mood, Glenn Miller Orchestra, 1940.

This Land is Your Land, Woody Guthrie, 1940.

Talkin' Union, Almanac Singers, 1941.

Nancy with the Laughing Face, Frank Sinatra, 1945.

Contemporary Literature

The Grapes of Wrath, John Steinbeck, 1940.

For Whom the Bell Tolls, Ernest Hemingway, 1940.

Berlin Diary, William L. Shirer, 1941.

Strange Fruit, Lillian Smith, 1944.

The Naked and the Dead, Norman Mailer, 1948.

Websites

A-Bomb WWW Museum
http://www.csi.ad.jp/ABOMB/index.html

Soldiers tell their stories
http://www.storypreservation.com/links-mh.html#WWII

INDEX

ACKNOWLEDGMENTS

The author and publishers wish to thank the following for permission to reproduce copyright material:

The Bettmann Archive: 582, 584, 594, 605, 606, 608, 611, 613, 614, 623, 635, 638, 640, 646, 661, 667, 669, 670, 683, 685, 688, 691, 692, 693, 694, 695, 701, 702, 705, 710; Bridgeman Art Library/Jackson Pollock/DACS 1995: 680; Culver Pictures Inc: 615, 644, 658; The Granger Collection, New York: 587, 593, 601, 602, 647, 704; Peter Newark's American Pictures: 653, 663, 673, 690, 699; Peter Newark's Military Pictures: *frontispiece*, 592, 597, 609; Popperfoto: 586; Springer/Bettmann Film Archive: 687; UPI/Bettmann: 589, 595, 598, 600, 607, 619, 620, 626, 628, 629, 631, 633, 645, 651, 652, 656, 657, 665, 668, 671, 674, 675, 676, 678, 682, 689, 697, 700, 708, 709, 712; UPI/Bettmann Newsphotos: 585, 622, 641, 648, 649, 650, 654, 655, 659, 660, 679, 683, 684, 707.

The illustrations on pages 590, 604, 607 (upper), and 642 are by Rafi Mohammed.

Page numbers in *italic* indicate picture; page numbers in **bold** indicate biography